Bought this one year - our early ones w. Pat + Tom -
Pat + I tried the Simon recipes we tried - the Autumn
Bisque + Walnut Meringues to much satisfaction :)

W9-BXX-853

gadabout, *noun*: a person who travels
often or to many different places, esp.
for pleasure.

—*The Random House Dictionary
of the English Language*

GADABOUTS

Cookbook & Travel Guide

Garlic Press

A Very Special Thanks to Bruce L. Roberts

Recently retired from J. P. Morgan, where he was vice president for Corporate Communication, Bruce Roberts just moved to New London with his new bride, Marie, and hoped to relax for a while. However, we at Garlic Press complicated his life a bit as we corralled him, then conscripted him, to edit this book. Bruce turned out to have the fastest mind and the fastest blue pencil in the East and made it possible for us to publish our book properly in a timely manner. We can't thank Bruce enough for all the help and advice he has given us; he has been peerless throughout.

Copyright © 1992 by Richard M. Leach and Catherine Utera

All rights reserved. No part of this book may be reproduced in any form without written permission from the publisher.

Published by Garlic Press, P.O. Box 222, New London, NH 03257

Orders and Customer Service:
(603) 763-9191
Facsimile (603) 763-5959

First Edition, First Printing
Printed in the United States of America by Graphic Litho Corporation
Illustrated by Nancy Begin
Book Design by Edith Crocker, DeFrancis Studio
Index by Nancy Crompton

ISBN: 0-9633069-2-8 Eggs in glass bowl
ISBN: 0-9633069-3-6 Dartmouth Hall

"Eggs in glass bowl" cover courtesy Simon Pearce
"Dartmouth Hall" cover courtesy Adrian N. Bouchard

Photographs pages iv and 281 courtesy Vermont Travel Division

"GADABOUTS" is a trademark of Garlic Press, New London, NH

Contents

Preface

The idea for writing this book was born during a holiday cocktail party at the world headquarters of Garlic Press. A guest asked, "Where's a good place for dinner around here?" There was a chorus of answers, and all mentioned different inns and restaurants. What's more, many had never heard of half the names being bandied about. It soon became apparent there was a desire and a need for a good guide to the area, and we decided on the spot to give birth to *Gadabouts*.

We expanded the restaurant and country inn idea to include descriptions of many of the towns and fun things to do in the Upper Connecticut River Valley and surrounding areas. You may find it surprising that there are so many hidden treasures and pleasures here; therefore we planned this book to help guide you through your adventures with our collection of maps, words, illustrations, and photographs.

We asked the chefs in our area to share their favorite recipes with you. We hope you appreciate that we did not alter their many different cooking styles. In fact, we think this makes the recipes fun and interesting; we've poked our noses into their kitchens for you.

Our goal is twofold: that you will enjoy the recipes, and that you will enjoy visiting the many wonderful places we have featured. Have fun!

RICHARD M. LEACH, a former Air Force pilot and for 25 years a Boston banker, moved to New London, New Hampshire five years ago, and is now head of a private investment banking company. He and his wife have seven children, and live in a hilltop home they built when they moved to the Granite State.

CATHERINE CROMPTON UTERA, who comes from a family of authors, spent seven years as a mechanical engineer in Boston before turning her attention to publishing and art. She recently moved to New London, where she lives with her husband and their two cats.

Foreword

New England has always invited words of acclaim for its beauty and charm as well as for its many attractions as a place to visit and explore. And nowhere are the quaint villages, rolling mountain vistas, and pleasing inns of the region more enjoyable to the visitor than in the idyllic areas of Vermont and New Hampshire captured through the words and pictures of this unique book created by Dick Leach and Cate Utera.

It's all here—the lovely clapboard houses, white churches with their distinctive New England spires, unusual shops, great restaurants, and friendly inns, in towns that are older than the United States of America itself. It's a simply wonderful area, and the authors have put together an informative and entertaining guide featuring descriptions of top visitor attractions and fun things to do as well as mouth-watering recipes by the most renowned chefs of the region.

I especially like the way the recipes, ranging from soups to sinful desserts, are presented. They make good use of indigenous products which are readily available, and can be followed by the casual cook as well as the more serious kitchen artist.

Dick and Cate are to be congratulated for evoking so much of the enjoyment offered by the natural beauty, rich resources, and hospitable people of this bequiling part of the world.

Francis Voigt
Chief Executive Officer
New England Culinary Institute
July 16, 1992

SOUPS & STARTERS

Asparagus & Sorrel
Vichysoisse
Autumn Bisque
Butternut Squash Bisque
    with Sweet Red
    Pepper Coulis
    & Fresh Cilantro
French Mushroom Soup
Chilled Beet Soup
    with Raspberry
    Vinegar
Czechoslovakian
    Cabbage Soup
Curried Pumpkin Soup
Tomato Garlic Soup
Gazpacho
Lemon Garlic Chicken
    Soup (Broth)
    For Colds
Oriental Soup Broth
Butternut & Acorn
    Squash Soup
Red Potato, Corn,
    & Oyster Chowder

Carrot & Honey Bisque
Pumpkin Bisque
Beet & Bean Soup
Roasted Corn
    & Basil Fritters
Pasta & Bean Soup
Ivy Grill East
    Buffalo Wings
New England Seafood
    Chowder
Mushroom Pâté
Bruschetta with Grill-
    Roasted Red Pepper
    Strips & Black
    Olive Purée
Fresh Mozzarella
    with Roasted
    Garlic & Coppa
Stuffed Mushroom Caps
    with Spinach, Bacon,
    & Crabmeat
Molly's Chili Relleños
Stuffed Mushroom Caps
Cheese Dip

Asparagus & Sorrel Vichysoisse

Discard white ends of asparagus and chop the remaining stalks. Trim the leeks saving the white bottoms. Wash thoroughly and chop. Peel potato and cut into 1-inch cubes.

In a heavy bottom sauce pot, heat the clarified butter over medium heat. Add leeks and asparagus and gently sauté for 10 minutes until slightly browned. Reduce heat and add flour. Cook 5 minutes more, stirring occasionally. Add chicken broth and bring to boil. Add potato and simmer 15 minutes. Add cream and simmer 5 minutes. Remove soup from heat. Add salt and pepper as desired.

Add sorrel leaves and purée in blender. Strain through a sieve and serve warm or chilled. Garnish with chopped chives if desired.

The Prince & The Pauper

SERVES 4

4 cups chicken broth
1 cup heavy cream
1 pound asparagus
2 leeks
Salt and pepper
1 medium Idaho potato
¼ cup chopped sorrel
*   leaves*
Salt and pepper
2 tablespoons clarified
*   butter*
2 tablespoons flour

THIS IS A WONDERFUL SUMMER SOUP THAT MAY BE SERVED EITHER HOT OR CHILLED.

Autumn Bisque

SERVES 4

2½ pounds butternut
  squash
1 onion
1 carrot
1 stalk celery
2 tablespoons butter
5 cups chicken stock
½ teaspoon salt
¼ teaspoon ground
  ginger
¼ teaspoon ground
  pepper
1½ cups light cream

Peel and seed squash and cut into 1-inch cubes. Add chopped onion, carrot, and celery to melted butter in a 4-quart saucepan.

Sauté until onion is transparent and carrot and celery is wilted. Add squash, chicken stock, and salt. Bring to boil, cover, reduce heat, and cook for 40 to 50 minutes or until squash is tender. Add ginger and pepper. Purée in blender or food processor. Add cream, reheat, and serve with a dash of whipped cream.

Pleasant Lake Inn

Butternut Squash Bisque with Sweet Red Pepper Coulis & Fresh Cilantro

SERVES 8 TO 10

2 large white onions,
  minced
4 cloves garlic, minced
3 ribs celery, minced
Butter or olive oil
2 large butternut squash,
  peeled and cubed
6 to 8 cups chicken stock
½ cup fresh parsley,
  minced
4 sweet red bell peppers
Fresh cilantro for garnish

Preheat oven to 350°F. Sauté onions, garlic, and celery in butter or oil until soft. Add squash and chicken stock, and simmer approximately 30 minutes until squash is soft. Purée in blender with parsley until smooth.

Roast peppers for 30 minutes, or until soft. Seed and peel, and strain through a fine sieve to make coulis.

To serve, drizzle coulis over bisque and garnish with fresh cilantro. (Coulis is a thick purée.)

Seven Hearths Inn

French Mushroom Soup

Cook the onions in butter until soft. Add mushrooms and cook until mushrooms exude their juices. Sprinkle flour over mushroom-onion mixture and stir to combine well. Cook over low heat about 4 minutes without browning.

Slowly add the chicken broth, stirring to combine well. Add thyme, salt, and pepper. Simmer gently 15 minutes to blend flavors. Add heavy cream. Stir to blend, and simmer an additional 5 minutes. Serve with freshly chopped parsley.

Simon Pearce

SERVES 6

½ cup minced onion
1 stick unsalted butter
6 tablespoons flour
12 cups rich chicken broth
Pinch of thyme
3 pounds mushrooms,
*   thinly sliced*
½ teaspoon salt
Ground white pepper
*   to taste*
1 cup heavy cream

Chilled Beet Soup with Raspberry Vinegar

Add the coarsely choppped beets and onions to stock and simmer until vegetables are tender, about 35 to 45 minutes. Purée the vegetables in a blender.

Add the finely chopped cooked beets, the cucumbers, vinegar, horseradish, salt, and pepper to the purée. Chill well. Garnish with sour cream and fresh ground pepper.

Stone Soup

SERVES 6 TO 8

2 cups coarsely chopped
*   beets*
1 cup chopped onions
3 cups beef and/or
*   chicken stock*
3 cups finely-chopped
*   cooked beets*
1 cup finely chopped
*   cucumbers, peeled and*
*   seeded*
3 tablespoons raspberry
*   vinegar*
1 tablespoon grated
*   horseradish*
½ teaspoon salt
¼ teaspoon pepper

Czechoslovakian Cabbage Soup

SERVES 10 TO 12

16 cups lightly thickened
   brown stock or gravy
2 pounds beef short ribs
1 teaspoon dried leaf
   thyme
½ teaspoon paprika
8 cups water
8 cups coarsely shredded
   cabbage (1 medium
   cabbage)
Two 1-pound cans
   tomatoes
2 teaspoons salt
½ to ¾ teaspoon
   Tabasco pepper sauce

¼ cup chopped parsley
3 tablespoons lemon juice
3 tablespoons sugar
1 package or one-pound
   can sauerkraut,
   rinsed and drained
Carrots for garnish
Sour cream

In a roasting pan place brown stock or gravy, short ribs, and sprinkle with thyme and paprika. Roast uncovered in a 450°F oven for 20 minutes until meat is browned. Transfer meat to a large kettle. Add water, cabbage, tomatoes, salt, and Tabasco. Bring to a boil. Cover and simmer 1½ hours. Skim off fat.

Add parsley, lemon juice, sugar, and sauerkraut. Cook, uncovered, 1 hour. Remove short ribs from kettle. Remove meat from bones, cut into cubes, and return to kettle. Cook 5 minutes longer. Add carrots and serve with sour cream.

Hanover Inn

The Darmouth baseball team, departing the Dartmouth Hotel, c.1880.

DARTMOUTHCOLLEGEARCHIVES

Curried Pumpkin Soup

Melt butter, add onion and garlic, and cook over medium heat until onions are soft, about 10 minutes.

Add pumpkin, stock, all seasonings, and bring to a boil, then simmer for 25 minutes with cover askew. Add cream and heat to correct temperature. Garnish with grated nutmeg and thinly sliced scallions.

Stone Soup

SERVES 6 TO 8

6 tablespoons lightly salted butter
2 garlic cloves, coarsely chopped
1 cup chopped onion
2 cups pumpkin pulp purée
3½ cups chicken or vegetable stock
1 teaspoon curry
¼ teaspoon nutmeg
¼ teaspoon sugar
¼ teaspoon white pepper
1 cup light cream or half-and-half
Salt to taste

Tomato Garlic Soup

Sauté garlic in butter. Be sure you do not let it burn. Add sugar, tomato purée, chicken broth, and Old Grand Dad. Bring to boil and stir, then reduce heat.

Put in blender and serve with dollop of cream and chopped parsley.

The Inn at Weathersfield

SERVES 8

1 ounce sweet butter
1 ounce finely chopped garlic
3 large cloves
2 teaspoons sugar
1 capful Old Grand Dad
4 cups tomato purée
2 cups chicken broth
Salt and pepper to taste.
1 cup whipped cream
5 sprigs fresh parsley, chopped fine

Gazpacho

4 large tomatoes
1 large can V-8 juice
3 to 4 cucumbers, peeled
*   and seeded if cutting*
*   by hand*
2 peppers (red, green, or
*   yellow)*
1 bunch scallions, sliced
1 to 2 "toes" garlic,
*   crushed*
1 lemon, juiced
1 lime, juiced
1 jalapeño pepper
1 carrot
1 small zucchini
4 stalks celery, peeled if
*   cutting by hand*
1 bunch cilantro
¼ to ½ cup olive oil

༄

A NICE SUMMER BUFFET
ITEM OR ACCOMPANIMENT
IS TO MAKE A MOULD OF
GAZPACHO AND SERVE
WITH GUACAMOLE SAUCE.
THE RATIO OF GELATIN TO
VOLUME OF SOUP IS I OUNCE
KNOX GELATIN TO APPROXI-
MATELY I½ TO 2 QUARTS.

Clean, cut, peel, and seed all vegetables. If you want to dice by hand, use 5 cucumbers, peeled and seeded. If you have a grater attachment for a food processor or a hand grinder, or a Kitchenaid mixer, you need to cut vegetables to accommodate this.

The only vegetables you can grate easily are cucumbers, carrots, and zucchini. Green peppers are recommended because they are cheaper and readily available. Onions and peppers chop nicely with the regular blade in the food processor.

Grind, grate, or dice vegetables.

Combine all chopped vegetables in a bowl, add citrus, sliced scallions, garlic, salt, pepper, and V-8 juice.

Jalapeño may be added gradually so that you can control the heat—add ¼ of a pepper at a time, and check after 15 minutes to ½ hour. Don't add seeds, and use caution handling peppers, wearing gloves if you wish. Don't touch your eyes (or any other sensitive areas) because the oil from the peppers may not feel obvious on your hands (although some people have a burning reaction on their skin). It will become very obvious if you carry the oil to another area.

The easy way out is to use Tabasco; it blends well and has an obvious heat factor. This kitchen recommends using both jalapeño and Tabasco because the flavors are different enough and they both complement the soup.

Add oil if desired; this gives the soup more depth and palatability.

Hanover Inn

Lemon Garlic Chicken Soup (Broth) For Colds

Over low heat cook garlic in olive oil; do not brown. Add 2 cups of chicken stock, bring to boil for 3 to 5 minutes. Add remainder of chicken stock, lemon juice, and sage. Boil 1 minute. Garnish cup with grated cheese. Drink as much as you can.

Just before bed, go early, heat 1 glass of good red wine almost to tea temperature. Drink and crawl under lots of covers.

2 tablespoons chopped sage
1 quart roast chicken stock
Juice of 2 whole lemons
2 tablespoons chopped fresh garlic
2 tablespoons olive oil
2 tablespoons grated Parmesan cheese

The Shaker Inn

Oriental Soup Broth

2 large chicken carcasses,
  breast only
1 cup daikon radish
2 stalks lemon grass
1 to 2 cups winter melon
½ cup fresh peeled
  garlic cloves
2 large onions, peeled
  and quartered
2 gallons cold water

Everywhere I've traveled in the Far East I've been a big fan of the local soups. They are as varied as the street corners, open markets, and shops where they can be found. Served at all hours of the day or night they are a staple of life.

So we will start at the beginning, the basic broth or stock. What we hope to achieve is a strong but clear stock. It's important that all the ingredients be as "white" or "neutral" as possible, and that the water is cold.

The chicken carcasses should have all the skin removed, with or without the breast meat. Peel the daikon radish and leave in large pieces. Remove the tops and outer pieces of the lemon grass to eliminate as much green as possible (optional, found in Oriental market). Cut the winter melon in large cubes (optional, found in Oriental market).

Combine all the ingredients in a large pot, the heavier the better. Bring to a boil and immediately reduce to a simmer. Never cover stocks, as this causes them to get clouded and to lose their nice clear shine.

Taste periodically after 60 minutes of simmering. Remove after 1 to 1½ hours. Whenever you are cooking anything, a good watch point for when you are close to finishing a dish is that it will become more fragrant. The trick is to teach yourself how not to go too far and cook out the essence and flavor. We also don't want the flavors to become muddled by boiling. A variety of flavors will be distinctive if broths are not overcooked.

Remove from the heat and let cool. Use a rack or leave the pot on the burner so that air circulates underneath. This is called tempering. After cooling, skim what has risen to the top with a ladle and discard it. Carefully strain the broth, trying not to break up any of the vegetables or chicken. Remove the carcasses and set aside whole for another dish of your choice, maybe Creole chicken stew with steamed jasmine rice.

Use reserved broth to make any number of things; some of the many variations follow.

Reheat broth with sliced daikon radish and garnish with chopped scallion and cilantro leaves for a palette cleanser during heavier meals that use a lot of sauces.

Reheat and serve with any variety of chopped Chinese cabbage, lettuce, spinach, mixed julienne vegetables, or mushrooms. Garnish with sesame oil and oyster sauce. Mung bean sprouts are good too.

Reheat and serve with pea pods, shiitake mushrooms, bok choy, and cubed tofu. Garnish with sesame oil and oyster sauce.

Reheat and serve with baby shrimp or crab, rice noodles or pasta, a dash of fish sauce, and fresh chopped chilies.

Reheat and serve with the breast meat from the stock. Pull the meat apart, add some very thin egg noodles, chopped iceberg lettuce, and sesame oil.

Reheat to medium temperature. While stirring the broth with a set of chopsticks, slowly pour in some beaten egg; just whites of eggs for a low cholesterol diet. Don't boil the eggs. Add sesame oil and chopped scallion for a classic eggdrop soup.

Etc.,etc.,etc.

Powderhounds

Butternut & Acorn Squash Soup

SERVES 10

1 onion, sliced
1 leek, sliced
1 celery stalk, diced
2 cups chicken stock
2½ ounces water
1 ounce dry sherry or
    white wine
1 sprig fresh thyme or
⅓ teaspoon dry thyme
⅓ butternut squash, cut
    into 1-inch cubes
⅓ acorn squash, cut
    into 1-inch cubes
¼ cup heavy cream
Salt and pepper to taste
Pinch of nutmeg

To prepare, sauté onion until golden. In a large pot, combine sautéed onion, leek, celery, chicken stock, water, wine or sherry, thyme, and butternut and acorn squash. Simmer for 20 minutes. When squash is soft, process mixture in a blender. Add cream and spices and serve.

Home Hill Country Inn

Carrot & Honey Bisque

SERVES 4

10 large peeled carrots
1 clove garlic
2 tablespoons chopped
    parsley
5 cups chicken stock
⅓ cup honey
2 cups half-and-half

Cut carrots into 1-inch pieces, place in chicken stock with garlic and simmer until soft. Remove from heat, purée, fold in half-and-half, honey, add salt and pepper to taste. Garnish with fresh parsley.

Red Clover Inn

Red Potato, Corn, & Oyster Chowder

Boil potatoes in lightly salted water until tender. Cool, dice small, and reserve. Strain oysters and reserve juice and meat separately.

In a heavy bottomed 6-quart saucepan sauté bacon until cooked; add the celery, onion, pepper, garlic, and corn, and sauté until tender, about 5 minutes.

Add white wine and liquor from oysters to vegetables and reduce until pan is nearly dry. Add light cream to vegetables, and bring to a boil, stirring frequently to prevent scorching. From this point on it is crucial that you do not scorch; stir a lot and keep an eye on your temperatures.

Make a slurry of the corn starch and wine; that is to say, mix them well. Pour the slurry into your boiling soup and whip until it thickens.

Add the basil, reserved potatoes, and reserved oysters to soup base and bring to a boil, then simmer 5 minutes. Season with salt and freshly ground black pepper. You may prefer your chowder either thicker or thinner—if it's too thick add more cream, ¼ cup at a time, until you reach the desired consistency. If it's too thin add more slurry, 1 tablespoon each cornstarch and wine at a time, until you reach the desired consistency. Whatever you do, don't scorch it!

New London Inn

SERVES 6 TO 10

1½ pound small red
  potatoes, scrubbed
1½ quarts shucked oysters
  (fresh!)
4 stalks celery, diced
  small
1 medium spanish onion,
  diced small
1 medium red bell
  pepper, diced small
1 teaspoon finely chopped
  garlic
4 ounces bacon, diced
  small
3 ears corn, shucked and
  kernels removed from cob
1 cup dry white wine
Liquor from oysters
4 cups light cream
2 tablespoons corn starch
2 tablespoons white wine
½ cup chopped basil

THIS CAN BE SERVED AS A
SOUP, SERVING ABOUT TEN,
OR AS AN ENTRÉE
SERVING SIX.

Pumpkin Bisque

SERVES 6

1 cup celery, diced ½-inch
1 cup onion
1 large butternut squash,
*   peeled and diced*
8 cups chicken stock
2 diced peeled potatoes
Salt and pepper
2 tablespoon diluted
*   cornstarch*
½ teaspoon thyme
2 bay leaves
Pinch cinnamon,
*   nutmeg, clove, allspice*

Sauté the celery, onion, and squash in corn oil until the onion and celery are clear. Add the chicken stock, potatoes, salt, pepper, and cornstarch. Simmer until vegetables are cooked.

Add the thyme, bay leaves, and spices. Strain liquid from soup. Purée solids in blender and add back to soup. Bring to simmer. Adjust seasoning. Let cool and stand overnight to develop flavor.

Soup may be creamed if desired. Garnish with toasted diced pumpernickel croutons.

Hanover Inn

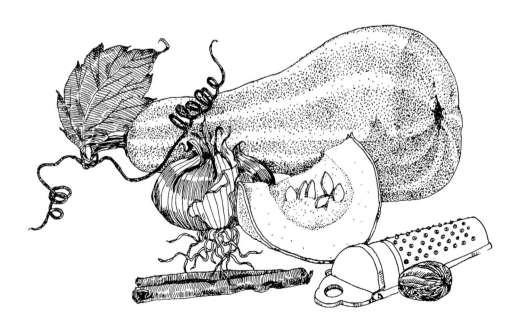

Beet & Bean Soup

Soak beans overnight. Combine all vegetables except beets (including cabbage), potatoes, and beans with stock; reserve beets for later. Add vinegar, salt, and pepper to taste. Cook until beans are done. Add beets and cook until done (or just heat through if using canned beets). Adjust seasonings, and cool to hand warm.

Purée in food mill or blender. Garnish soup with unsweetened cream whipped with lemon (add at end) or sour cream. Top with julienne snow peas.

Hanover Inn

SERVES 8

½ pound navy or great northern beans
12 cups chicken stock
1 cup each: celery, onion, leek white, diced ½-inch
1 to 1½ pounds fresh beets, steamed and peeled, or 2 cans beets
3 potatoes, peeled and diced
1½ cup cabbage, diced
Bay leaf
Thyme
Salt and pepper
2 to 3 tablespoons cider vinegar

Roasted Corn & Basil Fritters

YIELDS 50

Preheat oven to 275°F. In a food processor, blend first five ingredients. Add cold water and blend until smooth. Add corn and basil, and blend 3 to 4 turns.

In a large iron skillet, heat oil until very hot. Drop tablespoons of batter into oil and cook until golden on both sides. Keep finished fritters in oven while cooking. Serve immediately. (Note: batter will stay fresh in freezer.)

Seven Hearths Inn

3 cups flour
2½ tablespoons baking powder
3 eggs
½ teaspoon salt
½ teaspoon fresh ground pepper
2 cups cold water
3 cups corn kernels (6 ears corn), roasted
2 bunches fresh basil, chopped
Peanut or corn oil to cover skillet ½-inch

Pasta & Bean Soup

SERVES 8

1 cup dried pinto or
  white beans (cover
  with water and soak
  overnight; drain
1 tablespoon olive oil
1 cup chopped celery
2 cups chopped onion
½ cup chopped carrot
3 cloves garlic, minced
6 cups chicken broth
1 teaspoon basil
1 teaspoon marjoram

1 teaspoon oregano
1 large bay leaf
14-ounce can stewed
  tomatoes, chopped
½ pound dry Ditalini
  (macaroni), cooked
  al dente
Parmesan cheese
Pepper to taste

In a large saucepan sauté celery, onion, carrot, and garlic with olive oil until tender. Add all other ingredients except macaroni and cheese. Bring to a boil in a covered pan and simmer until beans are tender, about 1 hour. Add macaroni or pasta and simmer another 10 minutes. Remove bay leaf and serve with grated Parmesan cheese.

Pleasant Lake Inn

Ivy Grill East of Buffalo Wings

Day before party:

Cucumber Sauce: Peel and seed 2 large cucumbers and chop fine; grind or blend in processor or blender. Add 1 cup sour cream or plain yogurt, 1 teaspoon lemon juice, salt and pepper to taste.

Arrange 2 pounds chicken wings on a cookie sheet, pan, or casserole, and sprinkle with salt and pepper. Bake ½ hour at 375°F. Drain and cool. In a separate bowl combine: 1 cup soy sauce, 1½ tablespoons Tabasco, 1 tablespoon honey, and save for party.

Day of party:

Wings may be fried crisp in 1 tablespoon of oil or baked at 425°F for 15 minutes. Wings should be crispy. Drain excess fat. Place wings in bowl and toss with soy, Tabasco and honey sauce. Serve immediately. Wings can be kept warm in chafing dish if they last that long.

Hanover Inn

SERVES 6 TO 10

2 large cucumbers
1 cup sour cream or
   yogurt
1 teaspoon lemon juice
Salt and pepper
2 pounds chicken wings
1 cup soy sauce
1½ tablespoons Tabasco
1 tablespoon honey
1 tablespoon oil
Celery sticks

CUCUMBER DIP AND CELERY
STICKS SHOULD BE SERVED
AS AN ACCOMPANIMENT ON
THE SIDE.

New England Seafood Chowder

SERVES 12

1 cup celery
½ cup onion
1 cup bell pepper
1 cup potato
2 bacon strips
½ cup melted butter
½ cup white wine
1½ teaspoon thyme
  leaves
1 teaspoon tarragon
  leaves
1 teaspoon marjoram
  leaves
1 teaspoon ground white
  pepper
1½ teaspoon garlic salt
2 teaspoons garlic
  powder
¼ teaspoon ground
  nutmeg

½ pound fresh sole filets
½ pound fresh shrimp
  (peeled and deveined)
½ pound chopped clams
3 cups clam juice
2 cups water
1 cup chicken stock
1 cup flour
1 cup melted butter
4 cups cream
¼ cup dry sherry

Dice the first five ingredients. Sauté over medium heat in butter and wine for 5 minutes, stirring often.

Add the thyme, tarragon, marjoram, garlic salt, garlic powder, pepper, and nutmeg, and stir for 3 more minutes.

Add the sole, shrimp, and clams to cooking mixture. Then sauté and stir for 3 minutes more.

Add the clam juice, water, and chicken stock and bring to a boil. Reduce heat and stir in the roux paste made from the flour and melted butter. Mix well and cook for 5 minutes on low heat.

Slowly add the warmed cream; stir well, add sherry and let cook on low heat for 10 minutes more, stirring often.

Mountain Top Inn and Resort

Mushroom Pâté

Wash the mushrooms and cut into halves. Purée the mushrooms with the 4 cups of water in a blender or food processor. In a large saucepan, bring the mixture to a boil and then simmer for half an hour. Strain the mixture, separating the thicker mushroom portion from the liquid. Reserve the mushroom portion. Simmer the liquid again until it is reduced to about ½ cup. Set aside the glaze.

While the glaze is cooling, combine the remaining ingredients thoroughly in a mixing bowl with a paddle.

Add the thicker mushroom purée and the cooled glaze to the above mixture to make the pâté. The pâté can be refrigerated for up to 7 days. Serve with crackers.

Kedron Valley Inn

SERVES 10 TO 12

2 pounds mushrooms
4 cups water
1 pound soft cream cheese
¼ pound soft sweet
   butter
1 tablespoon fresh
   rosemary
1 teaspoon white pepper
½ teaspoon salt
1 teaspoon minced garlic
1 ounce marsala wine

Stuffed Mushroom Caps

YIELDS 24 CAPS

24 large mushrooms,
stems removed

Stuffing:
½ pound snow crab meat
½ red pepper, seeded and
finely diced
½ green pepper, seeded
and finely diced

1 small onion, finely
diced
2 stalks celery, finely
diced
1 tablespoon chopped
garlic
1 egg
⅛ pound melted butter
Dash salt, lemon pepper,
chopped parsley
Crushed Ritz crackers,
as needed

Combine all stuffing ingredients, except the Ritz crackers, and mix will. Add enough crumbs to make the consistency of a normal bread stuffing—not too dry!

Stuff mushrooms. Top with sliced cheddar or Parmesan cheese. Bake at 400°F until brown and bubbly. Serve immediately.

Lake Sunapee Country Club

Cheese Dip

2½ pounds medium
cheddar, finely
chopped
2 stalks celery, finely
chopped
½ cup onion
5 medium cloves garlic,
crushed

3 tablespoons
Worcestershire sauce
1½ cups sour cream
⅔ teaspoon black
ground pepper
1 teaspoon paprika
Dry sherry

Grate cheese, put in mixing bowl, and add all the ingredients except for sherry. Mix with dough hook. Mix well, then add sherry until dip has right (spreadable) consistency. Better if refrigerated overnight.

Barnard Inn

SALADS
DRESSINGS
VEGETABLES

Chicken, Snow Pea,
* & Cashew Salad*
* with Soy & Sesame*
* Vinaigrette*
Avocado Shrimp Salad
Chicken Salad
Warm Red Cabbage Salad
Basil Aïoli
* (Garlic Mayonnaise)*
Warm Kale Salad
* with Spinach,*
* Cob-smoked Bacon,*
* & Endive*
Fiddlehead Butter
Garlic Butter
Poppy Seed Dressing
Elaine's Peach
* & Pepper Salsa*
Tarragon–Honey Vinaigrette
Salsa Fresca
Green Tomato Relish
"Blue Front" Barbecue Sauce
Winter Purée
Garlic Mashed Potatoes
Tian of Vegetables

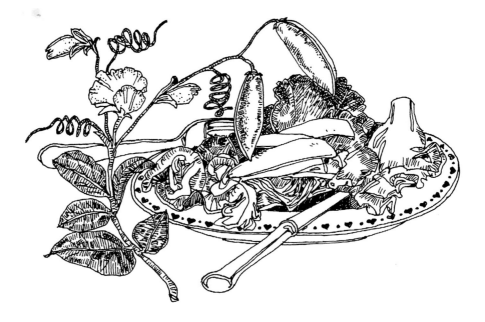

Chicken, Snow Pea, & Cashew Salad with Soy & Sesame Vinaigrette

SERVES 10

Soy Marinade:
1 cup soy sauce
½ cup sesame oil
½ cup scallions
1½ ounces red wine
vinegar
3 tablespoons minced
ginger
2 tablespoons sugar
1½ teaspoons garlic,
minced
Dash cayenne pepper

Soy and Sesame Vinaigrette
2 cups soy oil
1 tablespoon sesame oil
2 to 4 tablespoons
soy sauce
½ tablespoon
minced ginger
¼ tablespoon
minced garlic
½ cup rice wine vinegar
Combine and whisk

Salad:
10 three-ounce chicken
breasts, boneless and
skinless, or equivalent
amount of chicken
tenderloin, tendons
removed
2 to 3 heads lettuce
(Boston, red leaf)
50 snow peas, stemmed,
blanched, and shocked
Grated carrots
Water chestnuts or peeled
sliced broccoli stems
Alfalfa or radish sprouts
4 ounces roasted cashews
or toasted pine nuts

Marinate chicken 1 to 2 hours in the soy marinade. Grill, and let rest 3 minutes before slicing. Shred for salad.

For each individual salad, toss greens in 1½ ounces dressing. Mound in center of plate. Top with grated carrot, moistened with soy and sesame vinaigrette. Arrange snow peas in pyramid over greens. Alternate with strips of chicken and water chestnuts or broccoli stem slices. Surround with a thin ring of alfalfa sprouts. Garnish with sprinkling of chopped, roasted cashews. If no sprouts are available, substitute halved slices of cucumbers.

New England Culinary Institute

Avocado Shrimp Salad

SERVES 8 TO 10

8 cups cooked shrimp
2 cups finely chopped celery
4 peeled and chopped
   avocados
2 tablespoons chives
1 cup yogurt or sour cream

1 cup mayonnaise
2 tablespoons lemon juice
1 teaspoon vinegar
½ teaspoon salt
½ teaspoon garlic powder
1 teaspoon basil
1 tablespoon dill
¼ teaspoon dry mustard

Mix ingredients together in a large bowl. Serve on a bed of shredded greens. Garnish with alfalfa sprouts and a slice of lemon.

Peter Christian's Tavern

Chicken Salad

SERVES 4

¾ pound smoked chicken
   breast
1 can sliced
   water chestnuts
1 cup red seedless grapes,
   halved
2 stalks celery, chopped
1 teaspoon curry paste
½ cup mayonnaise

Cut chicken breast into bite size pieces. Add water chestnuts, grapes, and celery.

Mix curry paste and mayonnaise and add to above. Depending on the strength of curry paste, adjust to taste.

Gourmet Garden

Try!

Warm Red Cabbage Salad

Melt duck fat in sauté pan. Add prosciutto ham, sauté until starts to brown. Add cabbage and saute until soft over medium heat. Add walnuts and vinegar. Turn heat on high and sauté 30 seconds. Enjoy!

Corners Inn and Restaurant

❦

BRONZE MEDAL WINNER, TASTE OF VERMONT

SERVES 2

4 tablespoons rendered duck fat (or olive oil)
⅓ cup diced prosciutto ham
⅓ cup chopped walnuts
2 cups dried red cabbage
¼ cup balsamic vinegar

Basil Aïoli (Garlic Mayonnaise)

Clean and dry basil. Remove the leaves from the stems and chop them coarsely. Place the basil into a food processor or blender along with the garlic lemon juice, vinegar, and eggs. With the machine running at high speed, add the oil in a slow, steady stream until the mixture is almost the consistency of mayonnaise. Taste and season the mixture.

Garlic and Lemon Aïoli: Proceed as above except omit the basil and vinegar. Use 4 tablespoons of lemon juice instead of 2; and 2 cloves of garlic instead of 1.

The Shaker Inn

YIELDS ABOUT 4 CUPS

24 basil leaves
1 large garlic clove, chopped fine
2 tablespoons fresh lemon juice
2 tablespoons balsamic vinegar
2 whole eggs
3 cups olive oil

Warm Kale Salad with Spinach, Cob-smoked Bacon, & Endive

SERVES 4

1½ pounds kale green, stems removed from center
1 pound cleaned spinach
1 to 2 heads endive, sliced julienne
2 to 4 ounces slab- or cob-smoked bacon cut in ½-inch x 1½-inch julienne or lardoons
2 ounces sherry vinegar (or champagne vin egar with addition of 1½ tablespoons dry sherry)
1½ ounces peanut oil
Salt and pepper to taste
1 small minced shallot
1 lemon wedge

Arrange greens and endive on plate or plates. Render bacon 5 minutes to remove excess fat.

Whisk vigorously the vinegar and oil (blender or Cuisinart works fine also). Add shallots after mixed. Salt and pepper lightly. Squeeze lemon wedge.

Sauté bacon, drain excess fat. Cook to desired crispness. Carefully add cleaned kale and sauté (a wok would work best for this due to high sides). Thoroughly coat kale. Lightly salt and pepper. Cook until kale turns bright green and feels tender to the bite.

Hanover Inn

YOU MAY USE OTHER LETTUCES IF YOU PREFER, SUCH AS ARUGULA, MACHE, OAK LEAF. THE KALE IS HEARTIER AND HOLDS UP TO HEAT SO IT IS RECOMMENDED YOU ONLY SAUTÉ THE KALE.

Fiddlehead Butter

Sauté fiddlehead, leek, and onion in 3 ounces of butter until onions are translucent. Combine with all remaining ingredients in a mixing bowl.

The Woodstock Inn & Resort

1 pound butter
½ pound fiddleheads
(roughly chopped)
2 ounces chopped leeks
½ finely diced onion
¼ teaspoon tarragon,
thyme, and nutmeg

⅓ cup white wine
1 tablespoon Dijon
mustard
1 teaspoon raspberry
vinegar
Dash salt

Garlic Butter

Put all ingredients in mixing bowl and mix-whip to slightly fluffy. Keeps for two weeks in refrigerator or freeze in small portions.

Barnard Inn

1 pound unsalted butter
(room temperature)
4 cloves garlic, crushed
Juice of 1 lemon
1 tablespoons mustard

1 tablespoon
Worcestershire sauce
½ teaspoon black ground
pepper
1 heaping tablespoon
finely chopped fresh
parsley

GARLIC BUTTER HAS MANY USES
SUCH AS SAUTÉING SHRIMP, VEAL OR CHICKEN,
OR ON TOP OF STEAK OR FISH.

Elaine's Peach & Pepper Salsa

2 medium firm but ripe unpeeled peaches, cut into ¼-inch dice
¼ cup thinly sliced green onions
2 tablespoons minced red bell pepper
2 tablespoons minced green bell pepper
1 tablespoon fresh lime juice
1 tablespoon chopped fresh cilantro
1 tablespoon parsley
1 tablespoon olive oil
½ teaspoon ground cumin
½ teaspoon salt
⅛ teaspoon ground pepper
1 teaspoon (or more) minced jalapeño chilies

Mix all ingredients except jalapeño. Add 1 teaspoon jalapeño and cover. Refrigerate 30 minutes. Add more chilies if spicier sauce is desired.

Can be prepared 2 hours ahead, and refrigerated.

Hanover Inn

Poppy Seed Dressing

⅔ cup white vinegar
¼ cup chopped onion
1½ cups sugar
2 teaspoons dry mustard
2 teaspoons salt
2 cups salad oil
3 tablespoons poppy seeds

In a blender mix vinegar and onion. Add sugar, mustard, and salt. Blend well. With blender running, add oil and continue to blend. If oil rises to top, remove to bowl and mix with a wire whisk. Add seeds and blend. Keep in refrigerator.

Pleasant Lake Inn

Salsa Fresca

1 bunch fresh cilantro, stems removed
2 to 8 fresh jalapeño peppers, seeded and diced
1 carrot, peeled and cut-up
2 green peppers, finely chopped and seeded

4 stalks celery, finely chopped
2 or 3 scallions or 1 onion, finely chopped
6 to 8 fresh, ripe tomatoes, seeded and chopped
1 tablespoon fresh chopped garlic

2 tablespoons fresh chopped parsley
¼ cup lemon juice
⅛ cup cider vinegar
½ cup tomato juice
2 to 4 tablespoons tomato paste for thickening

Place cilantro, carrot, lemon juice, parsley, and vinegar in a blender or food processor and run until carrot and herbs are blended to a very fine dice.

Add all other ingredients to this in a stainless steel bowl and mix. Let sit refrigerated for 24 hours. Be careful of those jalapeños; they release their heat gradually. If not thick enough, add some more tomato paste. Serve with tortilla chips.

Lake Sunapee Country Club

"THIS IS A REAL FRESH SALSA THAT WILL BEAT ANYTHING YOU CAN BUY! THIS SHOULD COME OUT MORE GREEN IN COLOR THAN RED."

Tarragon-Honey Vinaigrette

In a large container measure all the ingredients. Stir or cover and shake well.

4 cups salad oil
1½ cups tarragon or cider vinegar
½ cup white wine
¾ cup honey

2 tablespoons finely chopped shallots
2 tablespoons tarragon leaves
1 tablespoon dry mustard
Salt and pepper to taste

The Village Inn of Woodstock

Green Tomato Relish

YIELDS 3 TO 4 QUARTS

6 pounds green tomatoes
3 medium size onions
4 tablespoons salt
5 thin slices of lemon
¾ cup finely chopped red
   peppers
1½ cup brown sugar
1½ cup cider vinegar
2 teaspoons white
   peppercorns
2 teaspoons whole
   allspice
2 teaspoons whole cloves
2 teaspoons celery seed
2 teaspoons mustard seed
2 teaspoons dry mustard

Wash and core tomatoes and peel onions thinly. Mix with salt water in plastic bowl, not metal. Let stand overnight.

In the morning drain thoroughly. Put tomatoes and onions in a large kettle. Add lemon slices, peppers, sugar, vinegar, spices, and mustard, tied in a bag (sheet). Bring to a boil and cook about 30 minutes, or until slightly thickened, stirring occasionally. Discard spice bag and turn relish into hot jars and seal at once.

Hanover Inn

"Blue Front" Barbecue Sauce

COMBINE
THESE INGREDIENTS
AND BRUSH ON
RIBS, CHICKEN, OR STEAK
FOR
A BETTER THAN
STORE-BOUGHT FLAVOR!

6 cups ketchup
¼ cup Burgundy wine
1 tablespoon celery seed
1 medium red onion,
   finely diced
1 tablespoon fresh
   chopped garlic
2 tablespoons
   Worcestershire sauce
2 tablespoons light soy

sauce
¼ cup Dijon mustard
¼ cup Wright's
   Liquid Smoke
½ cup Brown Pommery
   mustard with seeds
¼ cup salad oil
1 or 2 tablespoons
   Tabasco sauce
1 teaspoon white pepper

Lake Sunapee Country Club

Garlic Mashed Potatoes

Put potatoes in 1 gallon cold water. Add 2 tablespoons salt and bring to a boil. Reduce heat and simmer 20 to 25 minutes, until very tender. Drain well.

Add scalding-hot milk to potatoes in mixer with whip attachment going at low speed. Add garlic and butter a little at a time as well. Increase speed and whip until smooth. Pipe onto plate with pastry bag for special effect.

To roast garlic: roast whole bulbs of garlic wrapped in foil in a 350°F oven for about one hour.

The Shaker Inn

SERVES 10

*3 pounds boiling
     potatoes, peeled and
     quartered*
1 cup milk
*3 tablespoons roasted
     garlic*
*3 tablespoons unsalted
     sweet butter*
*1 tablespoon extra virgin
     olive oil (optional)*
Kosher salt
*Fresh ground white
     pepper*

Winter Purée

Blanch potatoes and celery root separately in salted water. Sauté the leek and the celery root in 8 tablespoons of the butter and then purée in a food processor. Add to hot blanched potatoes and mash or whip as you would for mashed potatoes. Season with salt and pepper, and add the rest of the butter and thin the mixture with some milk or cream as you would for mashed potatoes.

Hanover Inn

SERVES 6 TO 8

*2 pounds potatoes, peeled
     and diced into large
     cubes*
*1 leek stalk, white only,
     cut in ¼-inch slices*
*2 pounds celery root
     (celeriac), peeled and
     diced*
½ pound butter

Tian of Vegetables

SERVES 6

1 large eggplant
4 medium zucchini
  squash
6 plum tomatoes
1 small onion
2 stalks celery
2 clove garlic
1 cup grated imported
Parmesan cheese
¼ cup extra virgin olive
  oil
1 tablespoon fresh picked
  thyme or 2 teaspoons
  dried thyme
Salt
Pepper
1 tablespoon butter
1 bay leaf

❧

A GREAT ACCOMPANIMENT
FOR LAMB.

Slice eggplant lengthwise, then cut into ¼-inch slices. Slice zucchini at an angle in ¼-inch slices. Core fresh tomatoes and then slice at an angle ¼-inch thick and set aside.

In sauté pan add finely chopped onion, celery, garlic, butter, and bay leaf. Cook and cover until tender (approximately 4 to 5 minutes) then let cool. Spread this mixture in bottom of casserole or 1½-inch deep square baking dish. Starting at one end, arrange a row of zucchini up against the side of the dish. Next, arrange a row of eggplant up against the zucchini, followed by a row of tomato.

Repeat this as many times as you can, pushing each row against the previous one to ensure a tight fit. Sprinkle top with thyme and salt and pepper. Cover with cheese, then drizzle with olive oil. Bake covered at 350°F for 25 minutes. Uncover for the last 5 minutes.

Kedron Valley Inn

WOODSTOCK

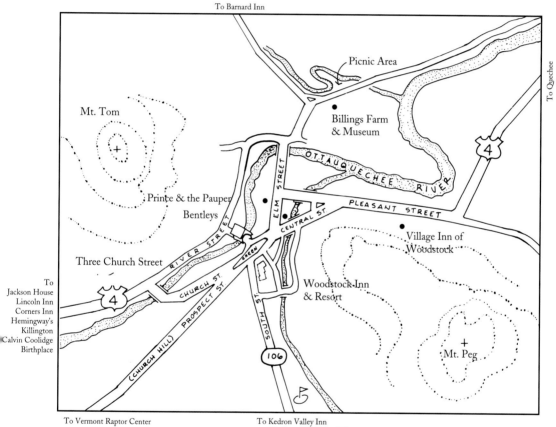

To Barnard Inn

Picnic Area

Mt. Tom

Billings Farm
& Museum

To Quechee

OTTAUQUECHEE RIVER

ELM STREET

Prince & the Pauper
Bentleys

PLEASANT STREET

4

CENTRAL ST

Village Inn of
Woodstock

RIVER STREET

GREEN

Three Church Street

CHURCH ST

Woodstock Inn
& Resort

To
Jackson House
Lincoln Inn
Corners Inn
Hemingway's
Killington
Calvin Coolidge
Birthplace

4

PROSPECT ST

SOUTH ST

Mt. Peg

(CHURCH HILL)

106

To Vermont Raptor Center

To Kedron Valley Inn
The Inn at Weathersfield

Woodstock, Vermont

Covered bridge in Woodstock

SPECIAL WALKING TOURS
ARE SPONSORED BY THE
WOODSTOCK AREA
CHAMBER OF COMMERCE
AND THE WOODSTOCK
HISTORICAL SOCIETY.
EVERY MONDAY,
WEDNESDAY, AND
SATURDAY THE TOURS
DEPART FROM THE
INFORMATION BOOTH ON
THE GREEN FOR A 1½ TO 2
HOUR TOUR. IT COSTS $2.50
PER PERSON.

Woodstock is one of New England's truly fine year-round destination resort towns, with everything you might want for that special Vermont vacation or just plain peaceful country living. Straddling the Ottauquechee River and nestled between Mount Peg and Mount Tom, the setting is spectacular. The town was settled well over 200 years ago, and in 1785 became the seat of Windsor County, which ever since has helped to draw merchants and professionals to the area.

Historically, because of its long distance from any major city, Woodstock had to be self-sufficient and produce and grow virtually everything needed to exist. Around the village green alone there were a thriving saddlery, hatter, tailor, baker, jeweler, two printers, tannery, tinsmith, two schools, two hotels, and over 25 other businesses, while on nearby Elm, Pleasant, and Central Streets more formal shops flourished. All sorts of industries sprouted up in the outlying districts, including saw mills and grist mills, a gin distillery, woolen mills, a brick kiln, and an iron casting furnace. Pottery, cooperage, basketry, and woodenware were crafted; a clockmaker, wheelwright, bookbinder, and carriagemaker plied their trades; and a comb factory and machine and tool shops sprang up. The manufacture of musical instruments ranged from flutes, bass viols, and drums to pianos. The town hummed, and the green also became the showcase of fine Federal homes that it still is today.

Toward the end of the 19th century the increase in railroading eliminated the need for much of Woodstock's self-sufficiency, and the area became less industrial. But its popularity as an all-season resort has never waned, and the town, and in fact the world, have never been the same since 1934 when the first rope tow ever was set up on a nearby ski hill.

In 1792, Richardson's Tavern opened to the public, and other inns and hotels succeeded it at the same spot on the green over the years until the 'old' Woodstock Inn opened in 1892. In 1897 landscape painter Arthur Wilder became inn manager, a position he held for almost 40 years. Thomas Edison, Henry Ford, and Presidents William H. Taft and Calvin Coolidge were some of the guests who stayed here during those days. Coolidge was a personal friend of Wilder and bought several of his paintings for the White House

In 1968 Laurance Rockefeller bought the inn, and the next year he and his wife, Mary, hosted a final dinner dance there. The old inn was razed and a new, modern Woodstock Inn & Resort was built on land behind. At the same time, the first authentic covered bridge built this century in Vermont, spanning the Ottauquechee River on the other side of the village green, was opened.

Today, the town's many attractions to visitors and residents alike include The Woodstock Inn & Resort's fine 18-hole golf course, ski-touring center, and Sports Center, the Suicide Six ski area, Vermont Raptor Center, Billings Farm & Museum, Woodstock Historical Society, Recreation Center and Little Theatre, Pentangle Council on the Arts, and Green Mountain Horse Association. Walking tours, hiking, shopping, and relaxing don't get any better than in Woodstock, and art galleries and antique shops abound.

Much of Woodstock's historic and environmental preservation can be traced to the dedicated efforts of George Perkins Marsh and Frederick Billings as well as the Rockefellers. Marsh, a 19th century U.S. congressman who was also largely responsible for the Smithsonian Institution, was the author of the ecologists' bible, "Man and Nature." Billings, builder of the Northern Pacific Railroad, purchased the Marsh homestead and reforested Mt. Tom and Mt. Peg, which had been laid bare by lumberers. The Marsh-Billings mansion is now occupied by the Rockefellers; Mary was Billings' granddaughter. They have perpetuated the tradition of environmental conservation and appropriately scaled commerce which still underlies Woodstock's economic vitality and outstanding quality of life.

F.H.GILLINGHAM & SONS, THE VERMONT GENERAL STORE, IS A WONDERFUL PLACE TO BROWSE AND SHOP. OWNED BY THE SAME FAMILY FOR OVER 100 YEARS, IT OFFERS A COMPLETE LINE OF HARDWARE, FINE WINES, SPECIALTY FOODS, AND MUCH MORE. IT SHOULD BE VISITED BY ANYONE EXPLORING AND ENJOYING WOODSTOCK.

Billings Farm & Museum

BILLINGS FARM
& MUSEUM

P.O. Box 489
Woodstock, VT 05091
(802) 457-2355

Open May 1–October 25
10:00 a.m.–5:00 p.m.

Also open November 27, 28,
& 29, December weekends,
December 26–December 31
10:00 a.m.–4:00 p.m.

Time to tour is suggested as
two or so hours

Adults $6.00
Children $3.00; under 6 free
and family rate is $15.00
(2 adults and their children
under 18)

SITUATED JUST OUTSIDE the village of Woodstock, Vermont, this is an enchanting place to visit for people of all ages. Great-grandparents to children will love this living museum of Vermont's rural heritage, where championship Jersey dairy cows have been raised since 1871.

In the museum, consisting of four beautifully restored, connecting barns, visitors will travel back a century ago to a time of hard work, simple pleasures, and the sustaining values of Vermont's hill-farming families. There are exhibits of a farm home, workshop, general store, ice cutting, stone wall building, plowing, and more. If it sounds dull, don't believe it for a minute. It is marvelously interesting to see what and how things were done in another era, and the presentation of exhibits is exemplary. Demonstrations of long-ago skills, including rug hooking and braiding, chair caning, and other handwork, take place daily.

The richly restored 1890 Farm House was built as a multi-purpose addition to Vermont native Frederick Billings' expanding farm operation, which had begun decades earlier. It contains a business office for the farm manager, a creamery, an apartment for the manager and his family, and an adjoining ice house. Nothing is roped off in this magnificent building so you can wander wherever you want, and there is usually a staff member nearby to answer any questions. Classic wood burning stoves, all different, are in each room even though the house was one of the first in Vermont to have a furnace as well as particularly interesting and elaborate indoor plumbing.

As you walk down to the dairy barn you see before you the hillside apple orchard, fields of corn, sheep and cows grazing against a backdrop of the rolling hills, and oxen and draft horses working here and there. Inside the barn magnificent pairs of huge Belgian horses live in the lap of luxury, one of the best Jersey herds in America resides, and, best of all, there is a nursery for the calves.

Seeing the herd milked every afternoon at 3:30 is a treat, and watching children, young and old, petting and scratching calves and lambs is a sight to make anyone happy.

Billings Farm was established in 1871 by Frederick Billings, a lawyer, businessman, and philanthropist as well as latter-day farmer, who was born in Vermont. He was one of the early "Forty-Niners," making his fortune during the gold rush, becoming the first person to practice law in California, and serving as that state's first Attorney General. He was also a leading conservationist, initiating the first reforestation of Vermont and establishing Yosemite National Park. As a railroad entrepreneur, he invested in the first northern transcontinental line, the Northern Pacific, of which he was later president. Billings, Montana was named for him. In the late 1860s he left the west, returned to Woodstock, and bought the old Marsh farm. Billings transformed the Marsh property into a country home and farm that reflected scientifically informed, progressive ideals of land use, reforestation, and agriculture.

Mary French Rockefeller carries on the Billings heritage of conservation in this generation. From her mother and grandmother (who was the wife of Frederick Billings), she inherited the commitment to land use that preserved the property through the early decades of the 20th century. With her husband, Laurance Rockefeller, she strengthened her commitment to conservation, joining a family that has made an enormous mark on the American conservation movement. Through the vision and guidance of Mary and Laurance Rockefeller, the Billings Farm & Museum is being preserved for generations to come as a working dairy farm and a museum of the rural Vermont heritage—a "do not miss" adventure for everyone.

✣

IN THE WINTER OF 1992, LAURANCE ROCKEFELLER, CHAIRMAN OF THE WOODSTOCK FOUNDATION, INC. AND FOUNDER OF THE BILLINGS FARM & MUSEUM, WAS AWARDED A CONGRESSIONAL GOLD MEDAL FOR HIS WORK OF THE PAST 50 YEARS IN NATURAL RESOURCE CONSERVATION AND HISTORIC PRESERVATION, AS WELL AS FOR HIS HUMANITARIAN EFFORTS IN THE FIGHT AGAINST CANCER. PRESIDENT GEORGE BUSH PRESENTED THE AWARD AT A CERMONY IN THE WHITE HOUSE. MR. ROCKEFELLER IS ONLY THE 97TH PERSON TO RECEIVE THIS HONOR IN OUR NATION'S 200-YEAR HISTORY.

Calvin Coolidge Birthplace

CALVIN COOLIDGE
BIRTHPLACE

*One mile east of Route 100
on Route 100A
in Plymouth Notch,
six miles south of US Route 4
Not far from Woodstock.*

*Plymouth Notch Historic
District
P.O. Box 79
Plymouth, VT 05056
(802) 672-3773*

*Calvin Coolidge's bedroom
where he spent his first night as
president after he was
administered the oath of office
by his father on the morning of
August 3, 1923, after receiving
notice of the death of President
Warren G. Harding.*

PLYMOUTH NOTCH, VERMONT, where the 30th President of the United States was born on the 4th of July, 1872, and first inaugurated in 1923, is considered the best preserved presidential birthplace in the nation. This rural village is almost unchanged since the mid-19th century. The homes of Calvin Coolidge's family and neighbors, the community church, one-room school-house, cheese factory, and general store have been carefully restored, and many have their original furnishings. The Notch cemetery is within a five minute walk; there, President Coolidge, is buried with six generations of his family. With true New England parsimony, the cemetery is located on a steep piece of land because the property is useless for any other purpose.

Perhaps this quote from President Coolidge, delivered at Bennington, Vermont, September 21, 1928, best conveys his feelings for this part of the world:

"I could not look upon the peaks of Ascutney, Killington, Mansfield, and Equinox without being moved in a way that no other scene could move me. It was here that I first saw the light of day; here I received my bride; here my dead lie pillowed on the loving breast of our everlasting hills. I love Vermont because of her hills and valleys, her scenery and invigorating climate, but most of all, because of her indomitable people. They are a race of Pioneers who have almost beggared themselves to serve others. If the spirit of liberty should vanish in other parts of the union and support of our institutions should languish, it could all be replenished from the generous store held by the people of this brave little state of Vermont."

Plan to spend several hours taking in this wonderful piece of American history. Visit the room in the family home where, at 2:47 a.m., August 3, 1923, Calvin Coolidge took the presidential oath of office from his father, Col. John Coolidge, a notary public. The then vice president had been vacationing here when word

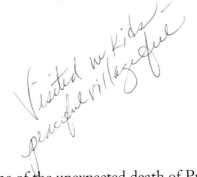
Visited w kids — peaceful villages que

came of the unexpected death of President Harding.

Also of interest is the room above the general store where President Coolidge and a couple of staff members conducted the affairs of the nation from this "summer White House." Just try to imagine that happening today! An interesting presidential museum nearby features Coolidge mementos and photographs depicting his early life and political career.

"BY GOLLY, YOU LITTLE RED-HEADED NEW ENGLANDER, I LIKED YOU." —WILL ROGERS ON THE DEATH OF PRESIDENT COOLIDGE.

The Coolidge kitchen, much as it was in 1872

VERMONT TRAVEL DIVISION

Vermont Raptor Center

VERMONT RAPTOR
CENTER

Church Hill Road
Woodstock, VT 05091
(802) 457-2779

VINS Visitors Center
Open summer
9:00 a.m.–5:00 p.m. daily
Winter closed Sundays

Summer
10:00 a.m.–4:00 p.m. daily
Closed Tuesdays

Winter closed Tuesdays and
Sundays

Adults:$4.00
Children: $1.00 (5-15)

☙

THE VERMONT INSTITUTE
OF NATURAL SCIENCE (VINS)
WAS FOUNDED IN 1972 AND
IS A PRIVATE, NON-PROFIT
MEMBERSHIP
ORGANIZATION.
THERE ARE MANY LECTURES
& PROGRAMS THROUGHOUT
THE YEAR FOR STUDENTS
AND ADULTS. SEND FOR
THEIR NEWSLETTER.

A RAPTOR is a bird of prey. Near Woodstock, Vermont, you can visit the largest raptor center in North America, now home to over 25 species of injured hawks, owls, and eagles unable to return to the wild. It is a fascinating place—you won't believe the size of a snowy owl (very large), and will thrill to see a bald eagle in flight—that is open to the public.

The Vermont Raptor Center is located at the Vermont Institute of Natural Science , west of Woodstock. To get there take Route 4 west; after you pass the village green turn left and then immediately right at St. James Episcopal Church and proceed up Church Hill Road for about two miles. The Center is on your right and you can't miss it.

Each year area veterinarians donate their time and energy to the Raptor Center's rehabilitation program and to the hundreds of birds of prey that are hurt in the wild. Most of them heal and are returned to their native environment. Those that are permanently injured, and cannot survive on their own, take up residence in the center's spacious flight cages where they can be observed by visitors year round. Birds born to resident parents are carefully introduced to their natural habitat and released. It is intriguing to watch these magnificent birds flying about their cages, eating a not-so-gourmet meal of rodents, or just sitting on a branch and staring back at you.

The Raptor Center offers self-guided tours, a very special opportunity to meet and learn about birds of prey in a unique environment. You can take all the time you want to study these beautiful residents of the center. There is plenty of open space, and picnic tables are scattered here and there.

The Vermont Institute of Natural Science also includes a 77-acre nature preserve with miles of wonderful nature trails. The gift shop is quite large and has many interesting raptor-related items to see or take home with you. This is not a great place to go on a rainy day, but it should definitely be on your list of things to do while in the Woodstock area.

Barnard Inn

FIVE OR SIX MILES NORTH of Woodstock on
Route 12 you will find the Barnard Inn on your right. It
is well worth the trip to this handsome 1796 farmhouse,
where the original owners not only farmed but also
operated a tannery and shoemaking shop in one of the
outbuildings. It is thought that this farm supplied leather
to the nearby hat factory that was in existence during the
early 19th century. Sepp Schenker and his family became
the owners in 1975 and renovated it for use as a restaurant
with major changes in the kitchen, lounge, and dining
areas. Otherwise the original brick structure is very much
as it was 200 years ago except for a front porch added
during the 1890s.

There are two gracious dining rooms in the front
that are perfect for small groups or for quieter and more
intimate occasions, while the large, fireplaced main dining room with marvelous old beams and antiques con-
jures visions of what it must have been like "back then."
There is an appealing lounge overlooking the gardens,
stone walls, and pastures beyond, and a big newer dining
room that is perfect for weddings, large dinners, or other
sizable functions.

The food is fabulous; Chef Sepp is renowned for his
peerless meals. His soups and chowders, smoked trout,
saucisse en croûte, or shrimp potpourri, to mention a few
of the appetizers, start the perfect meal. There is usually
a selection of ten entrees in the evening which might
include Vermont pheasant, roast crisp duck, veal
"Noisette," or various seafood and beef dishes. One of the
most memorable entrees is the glorious Chateaubriand
Cafe de Paris for two, cut at tableside and served with a
sauce made of butter, onions, garlic, mustard, and selected herbs. The dessert trolley is impressive and the
wine list is superb.

BARNARD INN

Route 12
Barnard VT 05031
(802) 234-9961
Closed mid–November
through mid–December
Closed April
Dinner only
Reservations should be made

Please don't
middle (and
the owners coffeecake
Nice touch on the yrs.
(Nice touches) over
the yrs.

Bentleys

BENTLEYS

3 Elm Street
Woodstock, VT 05091
(802) 457-3232
Open from lunch until closing

☙

BENTLEYS FLORIST CAFÉ

7 ELM STREET

(802) 457-3400

THE CAFÉ PROVIDES A
TERRIFIC COMBINATION OF
FLOWERS AND GOOD FOOD.
IT SPECIALIZES IN THE
"JUST PICKED FROM YOUR
GARDEN" LOOK OF FLOWERS
IN BASKETS, BOUQUETS,
AND BUNCHES. SOUPS,
SALADS, DELI AND SPE-
CIALTY SANDWICHES,
BAKED GOODS, BEVERAGES,
AND DESSERTS ARE ALL
OUTSTANDING. EAT IN OR
TAKE OUT. FREE DELIVERY
SERVICE IS AVAILABLE IN
WINTER.

BENTLEYS IS WHERE IT HAPPENS in Woodstock. Whether for dancing, jazz, good drinks, or good food, it is the place to meet, relax, and hang out with friends. The owners, Bill Deckelbaum and David Creech, have created the "hot corner" in Woodstock with this well thought out, vaguely Victorian restaurant, bar, and lounge. The small tables have flowers and candles to enhance the atmosphere and old prints, paintings, and photographs cover the walls. Large potted plants run amok, the lighting is intimate, and the background music is just right.

Bentleys' chef Joseph Burns, a native New Englander and graduate of the Culinary Institute of America, has incorporated his taste for contemporary American cuisine into Bentleys' menu. Luncheons feature homemade soups, renowned burgers, a wide variety of sandwiches, south of the border favorites, a selection of dishes including sausage crespoline and vegetarian quiche, and several cold plates. One of our favorites is the bayou chicken sandwich with a great spicy sauce.

Dinners feature Austrian pan-fried chicken, roast duckling, roast Vermont leg of lamb, Jack Daniels steak, and seafood. The Sunday brunch menu has many old favorites including classic eggs Benedict, which, along with Bentleys' "World's Best Bloody Mary," makes the middle of the day seem pretty special. Between Thanksgiving and Easter, Sunday brunch features jazz by several very accomplished local groups.

Out back there is a fabulous small intimate dining room with three tables. Upstairs there is an attractive Victorian dining room that seats about 35 at eight to ten tables; this is a perfect place for either a private party or a nice change of pace when eating at Bentleys.

Throughout the year there is dancing every Friday and Saturday night beginning at 10:00 and ending when it ends, and on Thursday and Sunday nights there is other musical entertainment. A nice assortment of hors d'oeuvres is served Monday through Friday from 4:30 to 6:00.

The Corners Inn and Restaurant

THIS FRIENDLY NEW ENGLAND bistro in Bridgewater Corners, Vermont, is frequented by knowing locals who sit at black, Naugahyde-covered tables gobbling up garlic bread under a ceiling of wood beams and hanging baskets. The bar, at one end of the dining room, is particularly appealing and is an ideal spot to relax and prepare for a delicious meal.

The establishment has won the Taste of Vermont medal, and the owners, Patti and Jim Gettis, have a flair for finding imaginative young chefs to prepare veal, chicken, sole sautées, and steaks, both grilled and broiled. Try the chicken breasts with escargot, the sole piccata, or thin fish slices dipped in an eggwash sprinkled with Parmesan cheese and sautéed until delicately golden and served with the bite of capers. Roast duckling and veal with artichoke hearts are other fanciful offerings.

An appetizer favorite (which won the bronze medal in the Taste of Vermont) is a warm red cabbage salad, tangy with balsamic vinegar, walnuts, and bits of prosciutto. Pastas take up half the menu, with interesting variations such as linguine with shrimp and a clam sauce that includes black olives, garlic, and white wine. Other favorites are veal chops, tenderloin of lamb with parsley, sage, rosemary, and thyme, and angel hair with seafood in a light cream sauce of sweet yellow peppers and sun dried tomatoes. The desserts are homemade and have been known to cause hoarding.

Sitting by the fire, enjoying the views and atmosphere, is an agreeable way to have a wonderful dinner.

Upstairs, for those looking for a casual country inn environment, are six bedrooms (shared baths) and a pleasant TV room.

CORNERS INN
AND RESTAURANT

Route 4
Bridgewater Corners
Vt 05035
(802) 672-9968

Open Wednesday–Sunday,
6:00 p.m.–10:00 p.m.,
seven days in holiday weeks

The Jackson House Inn

JACKSON HOUSE INN

37 Rte 4
West Woodstock, VT 05091
(802) 457-2065
Breakfast only

🙢

"AN ELEGANT INN SET IN
IDYLLIC RURAL
SURROUNDINGS."
—COLONIAL HOMES,
FEBRUARY 1992

THE JACKSON HOUSE INN OF WOODSTOCK is a landmark yellow Victorian house located a mile and a half west of the village. The owners, Bruce McIlveen and Jack Foster, purchased the building in 1983, spent a year and a half renovating it, and in 1984 opened a truly outstanding country inn.

All 12 guest rooms, including three suites, are furnished in different periods and styles of antiques varying from New England country to French Empire and Victorian. The only visible modern touch to the accomodations are the handsomely tiled or marbled baths.

Every evening in the parlor, wine and champagne are served along with a tempting variety of epicurean hors d'oeuvres (included in rates). On Saturdays and holidays a harpist plays themes from Broadway musicals.

Although dinner is not served at Jackson House, breakfast is a splendid feast with such delicious choices as baked apples stuffed with mincemeat, Santa Fe omelets, poached egg in puffed pastry topped with chicken in a sherry cream sauce, fresh smoked salmon on a dill biscuit with hollandaise sauce, and much more.

The natural outdoor beauty of this Vermont classic is a three-acre landscape of majestic trees, lovely gardens, a sculpture, brook, and flower-filled meadow. Guests who appreciate the privileges of living well are welcomed throughout the year.

Kedron Valley Inn

FIVE MILES SOUTH of Woodstock, nestled on 15 acres in a valley of the Green Mountains, is the Kedron Valley Inn, one of Vermont's oldest. The original part of the inn is the combination post office and tavern (now used as guest rooms) that was built in 1822. Six years later the lovely Federal-style main building was finished and has served as an inn ever since, first for stagecoach travelers and now for those who want to enjoy one of the finest inns in central Vermont.

The 30 guest rooms, all with private bath and cable TV, have beautiful canopy beds or marvelous old oak beds and impressive antique furniture and quilts. Many have either fireplaces or Franklin stoves. The congenial innkeepers, Max and Merrily Comins, emphasize comfort for all of their guests. The fireplaced living, dining, and lounging rooms are a pleasure to be in; hustle and bustle are not to be found here. The large front porch is a great place to relax with a book, a friend, a drink, or a snooze. And if this is not the place for you to unwind, try the wonderful large swimming pond out back with its spotless beach and splendid views.

For the past five years, the inn has been blessed with Chef Tom Hopewell in the kitchen. Tom's classical French training in Paris has inspired him to create a style he calls "Nouvelle Vermont"—nouvelle cuisine centered around local Vermont products and the freshest seafoods available on the east coast. Whether it's breakfast or dinner, you will know that the professional help in the kitchen is there to make sure you enjoy your visit and that everything at the Kedron Valley Inn is first rate.

Close proximity to Woodstock, shopping, golf, skiing, horseback riding, sleigh rides, and the other pleasurable "Vermont things to do" make this inn a delightful place to use as your headquarters.

KEDRON VALLEY INN

Route 106
South Woodstock, VT 05071
(802) 457-1473
Not open in April

⚜

"...MAX AND MERRILY HAVE TRANSFORMED THE HANGOUT FOR HORSEMEN INTO A VICTORIAN CHARMER THAT ATTRACTS THE MONIED CROWD THAT FREQUENTS WOODSTOCK. WHEN THEY'RE NOT STROLLING THE TOWN'S COVERED BRIDGE OR EXPLORING THE SHOPS JUST OFF THE VILLAGE GREEN, GUESTS OFTEN WANDER SEVERAL NEARBY HIKING TRAILS OR SWIM IN THE SMALL POND".
—YANKEE MAGAZINE, AUGUST 1990

The Lincoln Inn

THE LINCOLN INN

Route 4
West Woodstock VT 05091
(802) 457-3312

THIS INVITING INN is a beautiful, 200-year-old classic New England farmhouse three miles west of Woodstock on the banks of the Ottauquechee River. Here an interesting bit of Americana awaits the inquisitive explorer, for nearby you will find the only remaining wooden bridge in America of its kind. In 1844, T. Willis Pratt, the founder of The Pratt Institute of Design in New York, invented the bridge plan that bears his name. The design utilizes vertical wooden posts and crossed iron rods through the arched truss to the lower chords. This type became increasingly popular with the advent of iron construction and was the prototype of hundreds of steel railroad bridges still in use today throughout the nation.

Libby Francis and Chris McFarland, innkeepers, have created a wonderfully warm atmosphere in rooms with hand-hewn beams, cheerful fireplaces, and a well chosen collection of antiques. Relaxing by the fire in the friendly old library or warming up in the congenial tavern gives one the feeling of being in a delightful time warp. There are eight homey guest rooms with private baths and comfortable beds.

You always get good meals here; dinner at The Lincoln Inn is a fun experience. There is a nice selection of appetizers, soups, and salads. One of our favorites is a salad of smoked chicken, anchovy, grapes, hard-boiled egg, and greens called a Solomon Grundy, a Britishism of the old French "salmigondis" meaning a mixture. Venaison au chasseur—loin medallions prepared hunter-style with a sauce of tarragon, white wine, shallots, mushrooms and sauce Espagnole—is a preference of ours. Desserts are delicious and the wine list is inviting.

Canoeing in Vermont

VERMONT TRAVEL DIVISION

The Prince & The Pauper

THE PRINCE
& THE PAUPER

24 Elm Street
Woodstock, VT 05091
(802) 457-1818
Open for dinner year-round
from 6:00 p.m.

LOCATED IN THE HEART of Woodstock, down an alley just beyond Gillingham's, is The Prince and The Pauper—the best place in town for intimate dining. As you enter this delightful restaurant and turn left through the entry hall, you find yourself in an inviting little bar that makes you want to sit down at one of the half dozen tables and enjoy the surroundings. The bar itself is made from old hatch covers that have been varnished beyond the call of duty. It's also a special place to relax and enjoy the famous smooth and mouth-watering cheese spread.

The dining room is "L" shaped with tables in the middle and old wooden booths along the walls. The white walls show off the collection of wonderful old prints, while the dark beams, white tablecloths, burgundy napkins, and small oil lamps complete the inviting atmosphere. Chris Balcer, the effervescent chef-owner, prides himself in what he calls "creative continental" cuisine. The food is outstanding! For an appetizer try the house pâté that combines pork and veal with chicken livers, pistachios, and port wine, or try a soup, always first rate. There are usually six entrées that might include delicious fish dishes, crisp roasted Long Island duckling, veal, or beef. The boneless rack of lamb, first grilled, then baked in puff pastry with spinach and mushroom duxelles, is especially unforgettable. The wine list is perfect; you will find just what you want every time.

The Prince & The Pauper recently introduced a Bistro Menu in the bar that features equally delightful dining. If you are in the mood for a somewhat less expensive meal, yet every bit as tasty, or a featured hearth baked pizza, this is the place to go.

Three Church Street

LISTED ON THE National Register of Historic Places, this marvelous, three-story, brick and white-pillared Georgian dwelling is located at the western end of the Woodstock green just across from St. James Episcopal Church. Here Eleanor Paine, the owner, runs a very gracious and inviting bed and breakfast house.

The 11 tasteful bedrooms, six with a private bath, vary in size from cozy to luxurious, and some have fireplaces or Franklin stoves. Every guest room is different, with canopied double beds in some rooms and twins in others. The rooms on the Mount Tom side of the house overlook the clay tennis court, swimming pool, and Ottauquechee River and are our favorites with their large size and pleasing view.

The first floor has a wonderful sitting room with lots of books and magazines about for reading by the fireplace, or you may want to enjoy the evening news on cable TV. There is a large stately parlor with a handsome fireplace, grand piano, and lovely antiques at the front of the house that is splendid for relaxing and appreciating the captivating surroundings. This room, as well as the rest of the house, is perfect for wedding receptions and other special occasions. Three Church Street is well known throughout the Woodstock area for putting on delightful social functions.

The spacious dining room and back porch lead you out to typical Vermont scenery, with the lawn sprawling its way down to the river under the backdrop of one of Woodstock's two in-town "mountains."

Pets, children, and smoking are not frowned on here.

THREE CHURCH STREET

Woodstock, VT 05091
(802) 457-1925
Open year-round

The Village Inn
of Woodstock

THE VILLAGE INN
OF WOODSTOCK

41 Pleasant Street, Route 4
Woodstock, VT 05091
(802) 457-1255
Open year-round

THIS CHARMING, COMFORTABLE inn is situated on what was once a 40-acre Ottauquechee River estate and is within walking distance of the lovely Woodstock village green. A Victorian mansion, which is now the inn, and a carriage house are all that remain of the estate built by the Merrill family in 1899.

Throughout the inn the fireplaces and hearths, wood floors, rich oak wainscoting and mouldings, ornate tin ceilings, and heavy beveled glass are all original. Each of the eight guest rooms is agreeably furnished in country antique fashion with either quilts or chenille bedspreads on the comfortable beds. Some of the rooms have their original marble wash stands.

On the third floor, Dr. Merrill's billiard room was converted into two of the guest rooms. Downstairs in the cozy bar, stained glass windows, a 19th-century oak bar top, custom brass rail and fittings, and a nickel-plated sculpture add to the warmth of this gracious manor.

The dining room is a special hideaway for those wishing a romantic, candlelit setting. The inn's menu offers an appealing variety of fresh seafoods, milk-fed veal, beef, and poultry dishes. Also offered is a special New England treat—a tempting regional favorite varying nightly. Many of the guests return each year to savor the famous roast duckling a l'orange and roast rack of lamb as well as to relax in the inn's cheery ambience. The inn is open year-round except between the end of leaf-peeping and Thanksgiving.

The Inn at Weathersfield

DRIVE UP THE LONG tree-lined allée to this magnificient inn, cross the threshold into the keeping room with its wide planked floor boards, beamed ceiling bristling with dried flowers and herbs, and fireplace with a beehive oven, and you are taken back to a Vermont that hasn't been seen for many generations. This outstanding inn, with its 10 bedrooms, a bridal suite, and a family suite, has received praiseworthy press in just about every travel magazine there is. Each of the individually designed guest rooms, eight with a fireplace, is exquisitely furnished with period antiques. Beautiful four-poster beds, Oriental carpets, and sitting areas abound in this gem of a place to stay.

The innkeepers, Mary Louise and Ron Thornburn, exude hospitality as they offer each guest a piece of history. An open hearth is used on winter holidays for an 18th century gustatory experience. An internationally-recognized menu attracts guests to the antique-appointed, historic dining room or library. Ron, a musician of some repute, often provides piano music to grace dinner, while in the kitchen Mary Louise creates absolutely delicious meals to satisfy the pickiest of eaters. The white-clothed, candlelit tables glistening with all of the appropriate glasses and period tableware complete the captivating atmosphere.

Seven common rooms, including the sunny greenhouse, parlor, and living room, permit you to visit with other guests or just catch up on your reading or snoozing. Sit and relax on the Southern Colonial veranda or the porch facing the English perennial gardens. For the more active, the tournament pool table, volleyball, badminton, and croquet will keep you busy, and the spring-fed pond invites quick summer dips or skating in the winter. You may also use the aerobics exercise equipment and follow it up with a refreshing Finnish sauna bath.

There is a lot to do and see in this beautiful part of Vermont, and there is no more fun place to do it from than The Inn at Weathersfield.

THE INN
AT WEATHERSfiELD

Route 106 (near Perkinsville)
Weathersfield, VT
05151-0165
Tel. (802) 263-9217
(800) 477-4828
Fax (802) 263-9219

☙

"INN OF THE MONTH"
"IT HAPPENS EVERY TIME A GUEST CROSSES THE THRESHOLD INTO THE KEEPING ROOM OF THE INN AT WEATHERSFIELD: WITH THE HUGE STONE HEARTH CRACKLING WITH DRY LOGS, THE BURNISHED COPPER KETTLE GLEAMING IN ITS REFLECTED GLOW, THE LOW-BEAMED CEILING HUNG WITH ANTIQUE BASKETS, AND BOUQUETS OF FLOWERS AND HERBS DRIED AND ARRANGED, YOU KNOW YOU HAVE ARRIVED SOMEWHERE SPECIAL."

—COUNTRY INNS/B & B
MAGAZINE 1992

The Woodstock Inn & Resort

THE WOODSTOCK INN
& RESORT

14 The Green
Woodstock, VT 05091
Tel. (802) 457-1100
*   (800) 448-7900*
Fax (802) 457-3824

THE WOODSTOCK INN, beautifully situated overlooking the village green in the bustling, delightful town of Woodstock, is one of the finest resort hotels in the country. There has been an inn on this site since 1793 when Captain Israel Richardson, a Revolutionary War officer, built Richardson's Tavern for travelers and their horses as a place to eat, drink, and rest.

Laurance Rockefeller built the present inn 23 years ago and now there are 146 impressively decorated bedrooms, including three guest houses and seven suites, with 16 fireplaces scattered throughout. The mixture of antiques and reproductions throughout the inn is impressive, and a recent $15 million renovation left no stone unturned when it comes to making visitors comfortable. This newest version of Richardson's Tavern is a large and very comfortable place to relax after coming in from any number of nearby activities, including sports, musuem going, just wandering through town and its lovely gardens, or indulging in some of the best shopping in Vermont.

Thanks to Chef Peter Wynia and his talented staff, the food at the inn is superb. The menu changes daily and includes only the finest choices. The Saturday night buffet and the Sunday brunch are famous throughout the area; don't miss trying them, and plan to to spend enough time to enjoy the entire experience. The dining rooms are praiseworthy, the decor is handsome, and the service is friendly and professional. The inn was honored with "The Wine Spectator's Award of Excellence" for 1991; its wine lists were judged on the number of selections, quality of wines, depth of vintages, compatibility with the restaurant's menus, inventory, and how easy the lists are to use.

Facilities available to guests at The Woodstock Inn include cross-country skiing, an award-winning 18-hole golf course, tennis, squash, racquetball, and a sports center with a lap pool and full gym.

WOODSTOCK INN & RESORT

The main entrance of the Woodstock Inn & Resort

WOODSTOCK INN & RESORT

Aerial view of Woodstock, Vermont

Billings Farm and Museum from atop Mount Peg

BRIAN VANDEN BRINK

Over 50,000 people visited Billings Farm and Museum in 1991

JOHN GILBERT FOX

Percherons, Teddy and Sam, plowing at Billings Farm

JOHN GILBERT FOX

James "Pop" Lord, senior Interpreter, the greatest source of information about the barns at Billings Farm

JOHN GILBERT FOX

JOHN GILBERT FOX

Inside the General Store at Billings Farm

Farm Manager's residence

JOHN GILBERT FOX

Union Christian Church is located next to the Birthplace of President Calvin Coolidge

VERMONT TRAVEL DIVISION - TOM BROSS

The Coolidge Homestead is furnished as it was on August 3, 1923, when Col. John Coolidge, a notary public, administered the presidential oath to his son Calvin at 2:47 AM.

KINDRA CLINEFF

The General Store was operated by John Coolidge, the president's father.
The large room upstairs was used as the summer White House in 1924.

VERMONT TRAVEL DIVISION - TOM ROSS

THE INN AT WEATHERSFIELD

Main portico of the Inn at Weathersfield

THE JACKSON HOUSE

The Jackson House at Woodstock

JOHN GILBERT FOX

The Anheuser-Busch team of Clydesdales visiting the Kedron Valley Inn

VERMONT TRAVEL DIVISION

The Cabot Block in Woodstock, Vermont

Woodstock's Wassail celebration takes place each year just prior to Christmas.

WOODSTOCK INN & RESORT

MEAT & POULTRY

Beef & Guinness Stew
Steak au Poivre
Steak & Ale
Home-Style Cooked
    Beef Shreds, Szechuan
Lamb Meatballs with Spices
    & Yogurt
Lamb Tenderloin with
    Apple Cider Beurre Blanc
Rack of Lamb
    with Fresh Rosemary
Jesse's Peppercorn Steak
Medallions of Pork Loin
Roast Pork Tenderloin
    with Figs &
    Apple Brandy Sauce
Marinated & Roasted Rack
    of Lamb
    with Fresh Mint Jam
Fresh Mint Jam
Veal with
    Two-Mustard Sauce
Grilled Veal Chops
    Valdostana
Vermont Baked Veal
Veal Osso Bucco
Poached Veal Tenderloin
    with Fresh Herbs
    & Caramelized
    Vinegar Sauce

Medallions of Calf
    Sweetbreads with Morels
Veal Rolls with Cognac Sauce
Veal Tenderloin with Apple
    Slices & Orange Juice
Sauerbraten
Boneless Chicken Thighs
    with a Curry Sauce
Breast of Chicken
    with Glazed Apples
Baked Stuffed
    Chicken Breast
Boneless Chicken Breast with
    Cranberry Glaze
Chicken Breast Chalifoux
Oyster Chestnut Sage
    Stuffing
Chicken Lui Lui
Sautéed Chicken & Wild
    Mushrooms Served Over
    Polenta with a Rosemary
    Madeira Sauce
Chicken Valdostana
Duck Cassis
Maple Glazed Duck
    with Sundried Cherries
Roast Duck with Mango
    Chutney Sauce
Duck with Apple Cider
    & Ginger Sauce

Beef & Guinness Stew

In a flameproof casserole cook the onions and the garlic in 2 tablespoons of the butter over moderately low heat, and stir until the onions are softened. Transfer the vegetables to a bowl and reserve them. Heat the remaining 2 tablespoons of butter in the casserole over moderately high heat until the foam subsides, and in it brown the chuck which you have patted dry and seasoned with salt and pepper.

Add the reserved vegetables, the thyme, the sage, the bay leaf, the broth, and the Guinness stout. Bring the liquid to a boil, then simmer the mixture, covered, stirring occasionally for 1 to 1½ hours or until the meat is tender.

Discard the bay leaf, bring the liquid to a boil, and whisk in bits of the beurre manie until the sauce is thickened. Divide the stew and the potatoes between 2 heated bowls and sprinkle them with parsley.

Simon Pearce

SERVES 2

2 onions, sliced
1 garlic clove, minced
½ stick (¼ cup) unsalted butter
1 pound boneless lean chuck, cut into ¾-inch cubes
¼ teaspoon dried thyme, crumbled
¼ teaspoon dried sage, crumbled
1 bay leaf
1 cup beef broth
¼ cup Guinness stout
A beurre manie made by kneading together 1 tablespoon unsalted butter and 1 tablespoon flour

☙

OVEN-ROASTED POTATOES
ARE A GOOD
ACCOMPANIMENT.
MINCED FRESH PARSLEY IS
A NICE LEAF FOR GARNISH

Steak & Ale

SERVES 2

4 threee-ounce beef
    tenderloins
1 twelve-ounce bottle of
    Guinness stout
2 cups brown sauce
    (thickened beef stock)
2 tablespoons
    Worcestershire sauce
Salt and pepper to taste

Briefly sauté beef fillets in hot sauté pan with 1 ounce clarified butter. Remove to warm dish. Drain pan, pour in ½ bottle of stout, reduce stout by half, and add Worcestershire and brown sauce. Reduce heat and cook for about 5 minutes. Add stout or brown sauce to form a smooth rich sauce. Cook until medium rare for best flavor.

The Lincoln Inn

Steak au Poivre

SERVES 2

Two 10-ounce
    Delmonico
    center cut steaks
1 ounce brandy
1 tablespoon red wine
    vinegar
1 tablespoon Dijon
    mustard
1 tablespoon red currant
    jelly

1 dash Tabasco sauce
1 cup brown sauce
1 cup fresh cracked
    pepper

Lightly coat outside edges of steaks with pepper.

Brown steaks to desired doneness on both sides in lightly salted medium sauté pan.

Remove steaks from pan and deglaze pan with the brandy. Add the vinegar, mustard, jelly, Tabasco, and brown sauce. Heat and pour over the steaks.

The Vermont Inn

Home-Style Cooked Beef Shreds, Szechuan

Remove any fat or muscle from the beef. Cut into thin slices and shred. Mix with the soy sauce, cornstarch, and 3 tablespoons water, and marinate 30 minutes. Before stir-frying, add 2 tablespoons oil to prevent the shreds from sticking together.

Remove any leaves and peel the celery. Rinse lightly, drain and flatten with the blade of a cleaver. Cut into 1-inch sections. Diagonally slice fresh garlic. Halve red pepper, remove seeds, and shred.

Heat pan and add oil for frying, heat to 250°F. Add beef shreds and stir-fry for 20 seconds, until almost cooked. Remove and drain. Remove all but 3 tablespoons oil from pan and reheat. Add the chili paste, the garlic, pepper, ginger, and stir-fry until fragrant. Add the celery, beef shreds, 1 tablespoon soy sauce, vinegar, MSG, salt, sugar, cornstarch, and 1 teaspoon water. Stir-fry over high heat and remove to a serving plate. Serve.

Panda House

SERVES 6

*½ pound flank steak or
 sirloin
2 tablespoons soy sauce
3 stalks celery
1 teaspoon hot chili paste
1 stalk fresh garlic
1 tablespoon shredded
 ginger root
½ cup oil for frying
1 tablespoon rice wine
1 teaspoon black vinegar
 or Worcestershire sauce
¼ teaspoon MSG
¼ teaspoon salt
¼ teaspoon sugar
1½ teaspoon cornstarch
3 tablespoons water
1 red hot pepper*

Grilled Veal Chops Valdostana

SERVES 4

4 veal rib chops, 8 ounces
  each
4 thin slices prosciutto
  ham
4 ounces grated
  mozzarella cheese
1 tablespoon balsamic
  vinegar
1 clove garlic minced
4 tablespoons olive oil
1 tablespoon fresh
  chopped basil
1 teaspoon salt
Pinch black pepper

In a bowl combine garlic, vinegar, and basil. Whisk in the olive oil until slightly thickened. Add salt and pepper. Marinate veal chops at least 4 hours or overnight. Grill veal chops over a medium charcoal fire, about 5 minutes per side. Place the chops on a broiling pan and top each chop with a slice of prosciutto. Sprinkle with mozzarella and slightly brown under the broiler.

Works well with thick, center-cut pork chops too.

The Prince & The Pauper

GRILLED OVER CHARCOAL REALLY MAKES A DIFFERENCE!

Veal with Two-Mustard Sauce

SERVES 2

8 ounces veal cutlets
  (pounded thin)
2 ounces clarified butter
2 tablespoons tomato
  purée
3 ounces red wine
6 ounces very rich beef
  stock
2 tablespoons each whole
  grain and Dijon
  mustard, mixed
2 ounces heavy cream
1½ ounces white wine
  flour

Combine tomato, red wine, and beef stock in a small sauce pan. Reduce by half. Place clarified butter in large sauté pan, and get quite hot. Toss veal cutlets in flour and shake off excess. Brown both sides lightly in butter, add white wine, and deglaze pan. Add mustard, stock sauce, and cream. Reduce until fairly thick.

Simon Pearce

Medallions of Calf Sweetbreads with Morels

SERVES 4

1½ pounds calf sweet breads
2 tablespoons minced shallots
1 ounce cognac (or bourbon)
1 ounce port wine
1 cup morels quartered lengthwise (dried morels can be used after soaking in water for 1 hour or more)
½ cup veal demi-glace (or concentrated chicken stock)
⅓ cup heavy cream
1 tablespoon clarified butter

Blanch sweetbreads in boiling water with a splash of vinegar for 7 minutes, remove from liquid and let cool. Trim excess fat, membranes and ends, then cut into ½ inch medallions.

In a large skillet on medium heat, sauté sweetbreads in clarified butter with shallots and mushrooms 5 minutes on each side. Deglaze with cognac and add port wine, demi-glace, and cream. Reduce liquid by half on high heat, salt and pepper to taste, and serve.

Home Hill Country Inn

Vermont Baked Veal

SERVES 4

1 pound veal
½ cup bacon, cooked and diced
1 cup spinach, chopped
2 cups cheddar cheese, shredded
2 cloves garlic, minced
½ cup shallots, diced
2 tablespoons olive oil
Salt, nutmeg, and black pepper to taste
4 eggs
½ cup bread crumbs
½ cup flour

Cut the veal into 12 slices and pound lightly until very thin.

Stuffing: Sauté garlic, spinach, and shallots in the olive oil until soft. Add the cheese, bacon, salt, nutmeg, and pepper, and mix until blended.

Place ¼ cup of the stuffing on the veal and roll tightly. Dredge in flour and dip into slightly beaten eggs. Roll in bread crumbs.

Place on a greased pan and bake in a preheated oven at 350°F for 15 to 20 minutes or until golden brown.

The Vermont Inn

Veal Osso Bucco

SERVES 8

2 veal shanks
Seasoned flour
½ cup olive oil
¼ stick margarine or
    butter
4 sliced carrots
5 stalks sliced celery
2 large sliced onions
½ magnum Frascati
    white wine
1 No. 10 can or 2 large
    cans plum tomatoes
1 tablespoon garlic
¼ cup basil

⅛ cup thyme
4 bay leaves
Salt and pepper
¼ cup parsley
2 tablespoons beef
    base
3 strips lemon peel
Risotto (for 8) or
Linguine (for 8)

Toss 2 veal shanks in seasoned flour. Braise in cup olive oil. Add margarine or butter, carrots, celery, and onions. Sauté 8 to 10 minutes until slightly tender. Add ½ magnum Frascati white wine or any nice dry white wine and reduce by half. Add plum tomatoes, garlic, basil, thyme, bay leaves, salt and pepper, parsley, beef base, and lemon peel.

Place covered braiser in 350°F oven for 1½ hours. Skim off any fat and serve two shanks and vegetables over risotto or linguine.

Corners Inn and Restaurant

Visited W. Closet, Tod MCR + us for lunch + visited Sabra Fields ST. Glass window in Chapel at Dartmouth Hitchcock Hosp.

Poached Veal Tenderloin with Fresh Herbs & Caramelized Vinegar Sauce

SERVES 4 TO 6

2 each veal butt or whole tenderloin
2 sprigs tarragon, cleaned and chopped
2 sprigs thyme, cleaned and chopped
1 sprig rosemary, cleaned and chopped
4 sprigs parsley, cleaned and chopped
2 tablespoons shallots, diced
1 teaspoon black pepper
Zest from 1 lemon and 1 orange (optional)

Sauce:
1 onion, finely diced
½ cup carrots, diced
1 tablespoon butter
3 teaspoons sugar
¼ cup vinegar, white or red
¼ cup wine
3 cups stock or 2 cups brown sauce

Peel and trim tenderloins. Roll in herbs, pepper, shallots, and citrus peel and place on plastic wrap. Roll up and secure ends by twisting. Leave overnight.

Sauce: Sauté finely diced onion and carrots in butter. Add sugar and cook until dark caramel. Add vinegar and reduce until evaporated. Add wine and stock or brown sauce. Reduce and adjust seasoning. Thickeners may be adjusted with water.

To cook veal: Poach in seasoned stock for 8 to 10 minutes. Remove and let rest 2 to 4 minutes. Remove from plastic wrap and slice. Arrange on sauce. Serve with steamed broccoli buds and roasted potatoes.

Hanover Inn

Veal Rolls with Cognac Sauce

SERVES 4

4 to 5 ounces veal cutlets
1 large onion, chopped
4 cloves garlic, minced
3 tablespoons butter,
    melted
⅔ cup Italian seasoned
    bread crumbs
4 slices bacon, cooked and
    crumbled

Cognac sauce:
3 tablespoons butter,
    melted
2 tablespoons flour
1½ cups beef broth
¼ cup cognac

Preheat oven to 350°F. Sauté onion and garlic in butter until tender. Stir in bread crumbs and bacon.

Spread 2 tablespoons of mixture over each cutlet. Roll, starting with short end. Place rolls in a baking pan. Cover with tin foil and bake for 25 minutes. Uncover and bake an additional 10 minutes.

Serve with cognac sauce.

Cognac sauce: Add flour to butter. Stir until blended. Add broth. Stir until thickened.

Put cognac in a Pyrex cup. Flambé. Add cognac to broth mixture. Stir one minute. Serve over veal rolls.

Tulip Tree Inn

Veal Tenderloin with Apple Slices & Orange Juice

Bake tenderloins rubbed with oil and sprinkled with salt and fresh-ground pepper in a 400°F oven, uncovered, on a cookie sheet for 20 to 30 minutes.

Take sauté pan and put in orange juice, vinegar, apple slices, and spices to cook on high heat. Stir as it is cooking. Remove spices and apple slices when soft. Set apple slices aside. Mixture should be thickening. Add Apple Jack and simmer for 5 minutes.

Take veal tenderloins and slice. Place on hot platter, or individual plates. Add apple slices over meat and then dribble sauce over it.

The Inn at Weathersfield

SERVES 8

8 small veal tenderloins
3 Cortland apples, peeled
*   and sliced*
½ cinnamon stick
4 whole cloves
1 cup fresh or
*   concentrated orange*
*   juice*
2 whole allspice
1 teaspoon lemon juice
1 tablespoon Apple Jack
1 tablespoon vinegar
Canola oil

To: Remember Claire in NH!

Sauerbraten

SERVES 4 TO 8

2 to 3 pound bottom
    round or eye of round
2 carrots
2 onions
4 stalks celery
4 toes garlic, crushed
3 cups red wine
1 cup red vinegar or
    cider vinegar
1½ quarts brown sauce
6 bay leaves
2 tablespoons fresh or
    crystalized ginger
2 tablespoons cracked
    peppercorns
1 tablespoon thyme

Combine and marinate 4 to 7 days, covered. Remove from marinade, rub with Dijon or coarse mustard, salt and pepper. Sear in hot pan. Add marinade and brown sauce, cover and simmer. Cook 1 to 2 hours until tender like pot roast.

Strain sauce to use with meat. Garnish with root vegetables, braised red cabbage, and spaetzle or noodles. You may store in sauce for an extended period.

Hanover Inn

Boneless Chicken Thighs with a Curry Sauce

SERVES 4

4 boneless chicken thighs
    (approximately 6
    ounces each)
1 large onion, chopped
3 tablespoons butter
2 tablespoons flour
1 cup beef broth
1 tablespoon curry
    powder
3 tablespoons heavy
    cream

Preheat oven to 350°F. Cook chicken thighs in an uncovered roasting pan approximately 40 minutes.

In the meantime, in a saucepan melt butter. Add onions and sauté 10 minutes. Add broth and curry powder and simmer about 15 minutes. Add cream, stir about 1 minute. Serve with the thighs.

Tulip Tree Inn

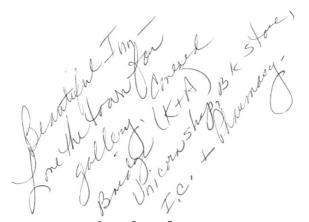

Breast of Chicken with Glazed Apples

Reduce chicken stock by ¾ in a sauce pan. Add the cream and salt and pepper to taste. Reduce by ¼ and whip in frozen butter.

In a small bowl blend mustard, eggs, and herbs. Season chicken with salt and pepper. Dredge in flour, dip in mustard. Roll in crumbs. Melt butter in skillet and cook chicken until golden.

Melt 2 tablespoons butter in sauté pan. Add sugar until dissolved. Toss apples until soft. Place the apples on the breasts. Nape with the sauce and serve.

The Woodstock Inn & Resort

SERVES 8

8 whole boneless chicken
    breasts, skin off
4 cups chicken stock
1 cup heavy cream
Salt and fresh ground
    pepper
½ pound butter, frozen
12 tablespoons green
    peppercorn mustard
8 egg yolks
12 tablespoons chopped
    fresh herbs (lemon,
    thyme, parsley,
    chervil, chives, etc.)
Flour and bread
    crumbs for breading
Enough butter to sauté
    6 large firm apples,
    peeled and cut in
    wedges.
2 teaspoons sugar per
    apple
2 tablespoons butter

Baked Stuffed Chicken Breast

SERVES 6

Stuffing:
½ cup salted butter
1 cup green pepper,
    coarsely chopped
1 cup celery, coarsely
    chopped
½ cup red onion, coarsely
    chopped
2 cups tart apples, diced
6 ounces veal sausage,
    coarsely chopped
¼ cup dry sherry
¼ cup white wine
1 teaspoon poultry
    seasoning
¼ teaspoon tarragon
1 teaspoon rosemary
½ teaspoon basil
¼ teaspoon ground white
    pepper
½ teaspoon garlic powder
6 slices whole grain
    bread, coarsely
    chopped
4 ounces grated sharp
    cheddar cheese

Stuffing: In a 2 quart sauce pan melt the ½ cup butter on low heat. Add the pepper, celery, onion, apple, sausage, sherry wine, herbs, and spices. Mix together and cook over medium heat, stirring often for 5 minutes or until sausage is cooked.

Remove from heat and add the chopped bread and mix until all the liquid is absorbed by the bread, adding more bread if needed. Set aside to cool. When the stuffing has cooled, mix in the grated cheese.

Sauce: Melt the ¼ cup of butter in a 2-quart sauce pan, then add the flour. Cook over low heat for a few minutes, stirring often, to make a roux.

Slowly add the chicken stock, whisking it into the *roux* until thick and well blended. Now add the nutmeg, cream, and sherry, whisking until well blended and creamy. Cook over low heat for 5 minutes, stirring often.

Keep the sauce warm until you are ready to serve. (If you prepare the sauce while the chicken is cooling, it will be ready at the same time. For a thick hearty sauce, double the amount of butter and flour.)

Chicken: Preheat the oven to 425°F. Lay the skinless breast on a baking pan, then pour the melted butter and wine over them, flip the chicken to coat, salt and pepper to taste. Bake for approximately 15 minutes or until the chicken is almost cooked. Then place ½ cup of stuffing on top of each breast and bake 5 minutes more until the stuffing is heated through.

Serve with the hot sherry cream sauce poured over the stuffing and garnish with chopped parsley and paprika.

Mountain Top Inn and Resort

Sauce:
¼ cup salted butter
¼ cup flour
1 cup chicken stock
   (warmed)
¼ teaspoon ground
   nutmeg
1½ cups heavy cream
   (warmed)
1 tablespoon dry sherry

Chicken:
6 six- to eight-ounce
   chicken breasts, skinless
⅔ cup white wine
2 tablespoons melted
   butter per breast
Salt and pepper to taste

Boneless Chicken Breast with Cranberry Glaze

SERVES 6

6 six-ounce boneless,
    skinless, chicken breast
    halves
Salt
Pepper
Flour
Salad oil

Glaze:
1 pound can whole
    cranberry sauce
¾ cup cranberry juice
2 tablespoons brown
    sugar
1 tablespoon cornstarch
1 teaspoon ground
    nutmeg
1 teaspoon marjoram
1 tablespoon minced
    onion

Salt and pepper chicken and coat with flour. Brown in hot oil. Reduce heat and cook slowly for 20 to 30 minutes, turning occasionally. Drain on paper towels.

Glaze: Mix sugar and cornstarch in a quart saucepan. Slowly stir in cranberry juice until smooth. Add cranberry sauce, spices, and onion. Cook over medium heat, stirring until mixture comes to a boil. Spoon over top of chicken.

Pleasant Lake Inn

Chicken Breast Chalifoux

SERVES I

Boneless chicken breast
2 tablespoons butter
¼ cup plums, peeled and
    quartered
1 ounce port wine
2 ounces chicken stock
2 teaspoons sugar
1 teapoon chopped
    parsley

Dredge chicken breast in lightly seasoned flour and sauté in butter. Add plums, port wine, stock, and sugar. Simmer until thickened. Finish with parsley.

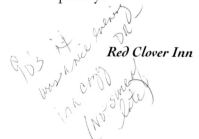

Red Clover Inn

Oyster Chestnut Sage Stuffing

Preheat oven to 350°F. In a large pan, sauté onions, garlic, and celery in butter until soft. In another pan, slightly poach fresh oysters in chicken stock, simmering approximately 2 minutes.

Bake bread cubes for 10 minutes, until crisp. In a large bowl, combine bread and melted spiced butter. Add oysters and stock, and remaining ingredients. Transfer ingredients into a buttered casserole and cover with foil. Bake for 20 minutes. Uncover and bake for another 10 minutes.

Seven Hearths Inn

¼
1½
2 cups
2 loaves
   cubed
1 loaf whole g
   cubed
4 large eggs, slightly
   beaten
2 cups coarsely chopped
   chestnut meat
2 bunches fresh sage,
   chopped
Salt and pepper to taste

Chicken Lui Lui

SERVES I

Flour chicken strips and saute in olive oil until almost completely cooked. Add broccoli and sauté 1 minute.

Add the rest of the ingredients and cook until cream is reduced by 80% (about 2 minutes).

Lui Lui

4 ounces skinless chicken
   strips
1 ounce olive oil
2 ounces broccoli
1 lemon wedge
½ teaspoon chopped
   garlic
5 ounces cooked rigatoni
1 cup heavy cream
Dash salt
Dash pepper

Sautéed Chicken & Wild Mushrooms Served Over Polenta with a Rosemary Madeira Sauce

SERVES 6

6 chicken breasts

Polenta:
4 tablespoons olive oil
3 teaspoons kosher salt
2 cups cornmeal
4 tablespoons butter
Pepper to taste

Sauce:
1½ ounces sliced domestic
    mushrooms
1½ ounces sliced wild
    mushrooms
1 teaspoon minced garlic
1½ ounces tomato
    chopped
1 ounce red pepper
    diamonds
1 ounce Madeira wine
1 ounce chicken stock
2 ounces butter bits
Chopped rosemary
Chopped parsley
Salt and pepper

Polenta: Bring 8½ cups water to a boil in a heavy rondeau (covered sauce pot with loop handles). Add oil and salt. Add cornmeal in a slow, steady stream, whisking constantly. After all the cornmeal has been added, cook over low heat until polenta pulls away from sides of pot (about 10 minutes). Pour into butter bread loaf pan. Chill and turn out. Cut into wedges and sauté to order.

Chicken: Heat sauté pan at medium heat and brown chicken, 3 to 5 minutes on each side. Then finish in a 350°F oven for 5 minutes on a sizzle platter. Wipe out and save sauté pan for the sauce.

Sauté slightly a wedge of polenta for each serving and remove to oven with chicken.

Sauce: In the saved sauté pan add mushrooms, pepper, tomato, and garlic, and sauté until tender. Add wine and stock to deglaze pan, and reduce. Add butter to bind sauce, add herbs, and season to taste.

Place chicken breast on wedge of polenta and serve with the sauce.

Cortina Inn

Chicken Valdostana

Debone and clean chicken breasts, discarding fat. Pound gently into a flat shape. Keep flat on the cutting board.

Sauté mushrooms in olive oil, salt, and pepper for 2 minutes only on high flame. Beat egg or egg whites with a pinch of salt and pepper and 2 tablespoons of water and set aside.

Heat butter and corn oil in a large frying pan. To stuff the chicken breast, place the Fontina and mushrooms in layers on one side (the inside) of a chicken breast. Fold the other side over, press down gently and seal with uncooked spaghetti or toothpicks. Dip the chicken breast stuffed and sealed into the egg and then into the bread crumbs. Pat the crumbs hard with your hands into the chicken. Stuff all four breasts and place into frying pan. Fry on both sides until golden brown.

Drain the chicken breast on paper towels for 2 minutes. The chicken breasts can be refrigerated for up to 1 day before baking. Preheat oven to 400°F. Bake for 25 to 30 minutes in a buttered or oiled baking pan. Serve with lemon wedges.

La Meridiana

SERVES 4

*4 fresh whole breasts of
    chicken
4 tablespoons sweet
    butter
2 tablespoons olive oil
1 egg or 2 egg whites and
    2 tablespoons water
Salt and pepper to taste
8 tablespoons Italian
    bread crumbs
4 ounces Fontina cheese
    from Italy cut into
    slices
4 ounces fresh mushrooms
    cut into slices
4 tablespoons corn oil*

Duck Cassis

SERVES 2

3½ to 4-pound duck
1 orange, sliced thin
Honey
½ onion
1 carrot
2 ribs celery
Anise or fennel seed
Port wine
Loganberries or red
  currants

⚜

A TWO-PART COOKING
PROCESS ASSURES A UNIQUE
DISH.

Remove breast from duck, and set aside. Cut leg and thigh away from remaining carcass. With a cleaver cut remaining bones into 2-inch pieces.

Breast preparation: Trim excess skin away from the breast leaving two-thirds of the breast covered. Score remaining skin in an "X" pattern. Brush honey on both sides, overlap with orange slices, and wrap in film. Leave at least four hours or overnight.

Cut up onion, celery, and carrot into 2-inch chunks. Place in small roasting pan or casserole dish. Add duck carcass.

Season leg and thigh with salt and pepper, sprinkle lightly with anise seed. Place in 300°F oven and roast for one hour. Remove to platter. Drain all the duck fat and reserve. Sprinkle 1 tablespoon of flour over bones and vegetables and stir. Add one cup of water and bring to a simmer for 20 minutes. Strain sauce and reserve.

Remove film and orange slices from the duck breasts. In a sauté pan add some of the reserved duck fat and heat. Place duck breasts skin side down into pan. Allow skin to crisp before turning, approximately 3 to 4 minutes.

Turn breast and cook an additional 2 minutes or until medium rare. Remove to slicing board.

Drain fat from pan, deglaze with port wine, add berries, then duck sauce. Slice duck breast thinly and fan slices on the plate. Arrange leg and thigh on the plate and cover with sauce.

Goes well with wild rice or roasted new potatoes, or your favorite vegetable.

Claude's

Maple Glazed Duck with Sundried Cherries

Marinate duck in ½ cup of maple syrup and ½ cup walnut oil. Reconstitute cherries in ½ cup warm maple syrup for 2 hours. Reserve liquid. Duck should be trimmed of excess fat. Cherries should be soft. Duck can be marinated the day before.

Heat heavy skillet on medium high heat. Place duck breast fat side down. Cook 3 to 4 minutes until skin is golden brown. Drain of fat.

Place duck in low 250°F oven to keep warm. Add shallots and marsala wine. Reduce by ½ on medium heat. Add duck stock and syrup from cherries and reduce by ½. Whisk in butter and season with pepper.

Slice duck and cover with sauce. Duck should be served medium rare. If you like it done medium, leave it in oven longer.

Kedron Valley Inn

SERVES 4

4 fresh boneless duck breasts
½ cup sundried cherries
1 cup duck stock (substitute chicken stock if none available)
½ cup marsala wine
1 tablespoon chopped shallots
2 tablespoons cold sweet butter
Cracked white pepper
1 cup maple syrup
½ cup walnut oil

Roast Duck with Mango Chutney Sauce

SERVES 4

2 five-pound fresh ducks
3 ribs of celery
1 large orange
3 tablespoons soy sauce
    with one tablespoon
    water
½ cup sugar
¼ cup water
½ cup white vinegar
Salt
Freshly ground pepper
Nutmeg
2 quarts duck stock
⅓ cup Zante currants
2 tablespoons duck fat
3 tablespoons flour
10-ounce jar
    Major Gray's
    Mango Chutney

Prepare ducks and stock a day ahead.

Ducks: Preheat oven to 375°F. Prepare ducks as follows: Open up cavity and remove giblet bag and neck. Remove excess fat from sides, cut off extra skin in back of wings. Trim off wings at second joint. Season inside of cavity with salt, fresh ground pepper, and nutmeg. Cut celery and orange into 1-inch pieces, stuff the inside of the ducks in a roasting pan. Arrange the necks and wing pieces on the bottom, in a fashion so that ducks will rest on top of them. Spread giblets in the pan as well. Place ducks on necks and wings and brush on soy and water mixture. Roast 3 hours, adding 1 quart of water halfway through roasting time. Remove ducks from oven, place them on a rack to cool.

Stock: Add 1½ quarts water to roasting pan. Place on a medium-heat burner and scrape bottom of pan with square edge spatula. Let stock come to slow boil and strain into container. When both ducks and stock are cool, refrigerate overnight.

Carve ducks by removing the leg and thigh portion, using boning knife along edge of cavity until reaching the joint. Carefully peeling thigh away from carcass, finish cutting off. Remove excess fat from inside of skin. Run boning knife along breast plate toward the wishbone. Cut wing joint all the way up to breast. Remove breast and wing bone in one piece. Remove fat from inside skin. Repeat on next 3 portions. Arrange skin side up on heavy sheet pan.

Sauce: Remove cold fat from top of stock. Reserving 2 tablespoons for roux in small sauté pan. Bring 2 quarts of stock to boil, add chutney and currants. Reduce to 1½ quarts at a slow boil. Meanwhile, in a small sauce pan bring sugar and water to a boil, cook until reaching a golden brown carmalization. At this point, pour vinegar in slowly, reduce by half and add slowly to stock mixture. Mix flour with duck fat and cook over very low heat for 8 to 10 minutes. Add to sauce and cook slowly for 10 minutes longer.

When ready to serve, reheat ducks in a 450°F oven for 15 to 18 minutes. Drain off fat once or twice during reheating. Place a thigh and breast portion on each plate and cover with sauce. Serve remaining sauce in sauce boat.

Simon Pearce

Duck with Apple Cider & Ginger Sauce

SERVES 4

2 four-and-a-half to
   five-pound ducks
2 teaspoons minced
   shallots
2 tablespoons clarified
   butter
1 ounce apple cider
   vinegar
2 ounces white wine
½ cup veal or duck demi-
   glace[1] or chicken stock
½ cup pure apple cider
   jelly
½ teaspoon fresh ginger
2 red apples, sliced and
   cored for garnish
Salt and pepper to taste

[1]Can be made by using
   duck bones, neck, and
   giblets.

Preheat oven to 500°F. To prepare duck, skin breasts, split, and remove carcass. Detach legs, removing thigh bones and all extra fat. Put duck skin aside.

To cook legs, wrap skin around exposed meat. Add salt and pepper and roast for 20 minutes. (Legs can be roasted ahead of time and reheated for 10 minutes in 500°F oven.) Let cool five minutes and place on a serving plate.

Place 4 duck breasts in a large skillet. On a medium flame, sauté duck breasts and shallots in 1 tablespoon clarified butter for five minutes on each side until golden brown. Remove from skillet and place in 450°F oven for 10 minutes. Deglaze pan with vinegar and wine. Add demi-glace and apple jelly and bring to a boil. Reduce by one third. Add ginger and boil for one minute. Strain sauce. Add salt and pepper to taste.

Remove duck breasts from oven and let cool for 5 minutes. Sauté apple slices in 1 tablespoon butter until golden. When duck is cool, slice lengthwise and lay out in fan shape near leg on serving plate. Coat duck with 1½ ounces of sauce. Decorate plates with apple slices.

Home Hill Country Inn

QUECHEE

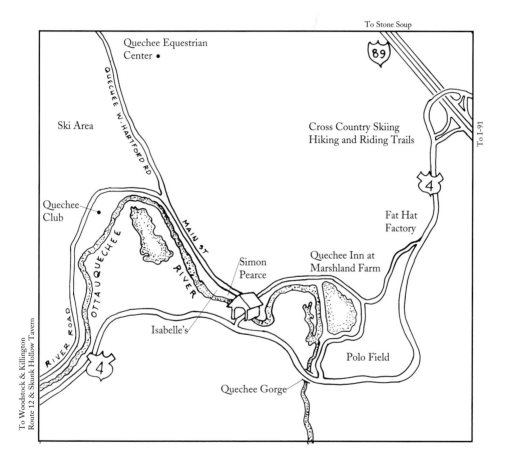

To Stone Soup

89

Quechee Equestrian
Center •

QUECHEE W-HARTFORD RD

Ski Area

Cross Country Skiing
Hiking and Riding Trails

To I-91

4

Quechee
Club

MAIN ST

Fat Hat
Factory

OTTAUQUECHEE RIVER

Simon
Pearce

Quechee Inn at
Marshland Farm

RIVER ROAD

Isabelle's

Polo Field

To Woodstock & Killington
Route 12 & Skunk Hollow Tavern

4

Quechee Gorge

Country auction in Vermont

VERMONT TRAVEL BUREAU

An active sugarhouse in Vermont is a sure sign that spring is just around the corner.

VERMONT TRAVEL DIVISION

SIMON PEARCE

LEFT: Whether dining inside or out, the views from Simon Pearce are always a treat.

RIGHT: The covered bridge at Quechee, over the Ottauquechee River, is but one of several ways to get to Simon Pearce.

BELOW: Golfing at Quechee is hard to beat. The Lakeside course is in the foreground while farther back is the Highland course.

SIMON PEARCE

HANSON CARROLL

VERMONT TRAVEL DIVISION

Quechee Inn at Marshland Farm

BARBARA J. WEST

Watching polo is a wonderful way to spend part of a summer weekend in Quechee

Quechee

This beautiful New England town on the banks of Vermont's Ottauquechee River is truly a marvelous all-season vacationland. Whether enjoying the recreational activities around town, or driving along scenic back roads in search of antique treasures or fine country dining, you'll find a visit to Quechee well worth your time.

Quechee Gorge State Park features the 165-foot deep, very steep, and mile-long Quechee Gorge with the river running through. This gorge is a wonderful place for hiking and picnicking and, although it never really seems crowded, is the single most visited natural attraction in Vermont. The Quechee Chamber of Commerce is presently upgrading and improving the walking trails through the gorge to make visits here even more pleasurable.

Antique shops are scattered throughout the area, and on Route 4 that runs through town there are two large complexes with many shops within. Antiques Collaborative at Waterman House, just up from the covered bridge in Quechee, and Timber Village, a little east of Quechee Gorge, each will give hours of browsing if you're interested in antiquing.

The Quechee Club, just outside the village, offers extensive recreational and country club facilities for members of the Quechee Lakes Landowners' Association and extends limited privileges to guests of nearby inns. The Association was formed over 20 years ago to protect and enhance the more than 6,000 acres of farmland and forest that provide the land for the 1,500 homeowners in the Quechee Lakes community.

The clubhouse contains a large indoor pool, squash courts, locker rooms, dining room, and lounge. The canopied deck overlooking the first hole of the Lakeside golf course, an outdoor swimming pool, and the river, is a special place for drinks and meals during the summer months. Two Geoffrey Cornish championship golf courses are served by the pro shop in this clubhouse. If you can get on one of these courses it is well worth it as they are

☙

GALLERY AT QUECHEE
2 MAIN STREET P.O. BOX 182
QUECHEE, VT 05059
(802) 295-3744
THIS MARVELOUS GALLERY
LOCATED ON THE LOWER
FLOOR OF THE EMPORIUM
BUILDING, UNDER
QUECHEE ASSOCIATES,
OVERLOOKING THE FALLS,
IS WELL WORTH A VISIT.
THEY FEATURE
CONTEMPORY AND NOT-SO-
CONTEMPORY ART FOR ALL
TASTES.

a good test of golf in a beautiful setting. Nearby there is a tennis facility featuring three all-weather courts and eight Har-Tru courts, along with a pavilion for watching tournaments or casual matches.

"Leaf peepers" have the time of their lives in this part of Vermont. Autumn is a very special season here and the Vermonters go out of their way to make visitors feel welcome.

There are all sorts of trails in Quechee for cross-country skiing, horseback riding, and hiking, and the facilities are superb. Quechee has its own downhill skiing area with a chairlift and a T-bar as well as snow making equipment. This is a great family skiing spot for those who do not want to make the trip to the larger resorts.

Horses are an important part of the Quechee scene, with polo matches almost every weekend during the summer on the polo grounds down near Dewey's Lake. The Equestrian Center, at the other end of town, has a large indoor riding arena and viewing gallery, a wonderful place to watch dressage and jumping, often to music.

In 1991 outdoor dressage to music was started in the summer on the Village Green. Seating is available under tents for a fee and hors d'oevres and wine are served. The proceeds in the first year went to the Vermont Institute of Natural Science, and the 1992 beneficiary is the Vermont Handicapped Riders and Skiers Association (similar to the Special Olympics). Quechee also hosts a three-day weekend during the winter for a Special Olympics skiing event that has become one of the area's great winter occasions. The Balloon Festival in mid-June and the Scottish Festival later in the summer draw many ardent fans every year and you will not be disappointed if you attend.

Band concerts take place on the Village Green on scattered weekends during the summer, and some are catered. Sitting under the stars on the banks of the river enjoying a concert in Quechee is a special way to end a day.

For all events taking place in Quechee it is best to call the Chamber of Commerce at (802) 295-7900 to make sure you are at the right place at the right time.

❦

THE BALLOON FESTIVAL IN MID-JUNE AND THE SCOTTISH FESTIVAL, LATER ON IN THE SUMMER, ARE TWO EVENTS THAT DRAW MANY ARDENT FANS EVERY YEAR.

VERMONT TRAVEL DIVISION

Annual Balloon Festival on the village green, Quechee, Vermont

Quechee Gorge

Isabelle's at Parker House

SET IN THE FORMER MANSION of Vermont Senator Joseph C. Parker, Isabelle's at Parker House in Quechee enjoys a spectacular setting on the edge of the Ottauquechee River in this beautiful village with its covered bridge, waterfall, white New England houses, and great shopping.

Isabelle's features a changing prix fixe menu. It might include fresh New England sea scallops with basil sauce for starters, followed by a spinach and endive salad, and then boneless chicken breast with sundried tomatoes or a rack of lamb with a thyme and rosemary sauce.

And Isabelle's homemade desserts will tempt even the most restrained of souls. A bistro menu, for those wanting lighter fare, is available in the very attractive and comfortable bar area that overlooks the river. Items such as smoked ham and melted brie on a baguette with Dijon mustard, or a salad of grilled chicken breast on a bed of spinach with curry vinaigrette, are just two of the many of the delicacies awaiting you. Outdoor dining on the screened porch is an attraction during the summer months.

The Parker House is one of the few small inns in Quechee. It has seven wonderful bedrooms, all totally redone and complete with full bath, with either queen or king size beds complemented by period antiques. There is a very pleasant common room on the second floor where you can meet with friends or just relax and read.

ISABELLE'S AT PARKER HOUSE

16 Main Street
Quechee, VT 05059
(802) 295-6077
Open from 5:30 p.m.
year-round

One afternoon we visited in the 90's. Quilts

The Quechee Inn at Marshland Farm

THE QUECHEE INN AT
MARSHLAND FARM

Clubhouse Road
Quechee, VT 05059
Tel. (802) 295-3133
(800) 235-3133
Fax. (802) 295-6587
Open year-round

THE QUECHEE INN AT MARSHLAND FARM is a superbly restored, 1793 farmhouse built for Vermont's first Lieutenant Governor, Colonel Joseph Marsh. The inn has been renovated and expanded with great care, including details such as wide board "pumpkin" pine floors and finishing touches like Queen Anne furnishings and multi-paned windows overlooking the pond. The inn is what you would expect a beautiful Vermont country inn to look like. Just across the road from the Ottauquechee River, it is a large, rambling white farmhouse with an equally large red barn at the rear, all set against an imposing mountainside.

There are 24 guestrooms, each with a different decor. All are comfortable and all have a private bath and cable TV. The newly done library, lounge, living room, and dining room are decorated in the classic New England inn manner. When weather permits, cocktails on the covered patio are particularly pleasant.

The food at The Quechee Inn is just what the doctor ordered; a large breakfast buffet starts the day and the impressive dinner menu should satisfy everyone. Executive Chef Kevin Lane has 20 years of experience in New England restaurants and inns, with his last five years spent here. A truly classic American gourmet chef, Kevin uses fresh local produce and herbs in season, as well as local meats and game. His favorite cooking is influenced by Italian and French cuisine.

There are plenty of other things to do at the inn. The Vermont Fly Fishing School is located here. The river in front is stocked with brown trout, and nearby White River is the spot for rainbow trout and smallmouth bass. Day trips in canoes start right at the inn, and golf is available at the Quechee Club with its two championship 18-hole courses. Tennis, squash, swimming, cross-country skiing, biking, you name it, are also available.

Simon Pearce

Every year with family or friends, never let us down.

ONE VISIT TO SIMON PEARCE is not enough, nor will we ever know when to stop going there. Fascinating things are always happening in this marvelous converted woolen mill, built in 1801, overlooking a waterfall on the Ottauquechee River. You can spend hours shopping for glass, woolens, pottery, exceptional things for "the table," furniture, lamps, and many other items to grace your house. It is hard to find something you don't want!

Downstairs there is a glassblowing area that is constantly alive with workers making many of the glasses, goblets, and pitchers you saw offered for sale upstairs. Around the corner you can watch a glob of clay being transformed into a lovely vase in the pottery shop, or go a bit further and see the water-powered turbine in the hydro station that provides all the power for Simon Pearce as well as a good part of the power for the village of Quechee. The pulse in this building never stops beating.

When you want to catch your breath and digest the beautiful products you've just seen, you must go to the restaurant for a delicious meal. The tables are set with tableware and glasses all made by the artisans at Simon Pearce. The wine list is superb. The menu is not long or complicated, but it's hard to make a quick decision, as there is so much that looks really good. If you eat at Simon Pearce frequently you'll soon discover that the quality of the meals is impeccably consistent—always mouth-watering and delectable.

In 1981, Simon Pearce, the man, came to this country from Ballymaloe in Ireland and bought the mill; in 1986 he started the restaurant. A lot of the people working here also brought their many talents from Ireland. Simon and his family and friends have taken this setting, with it's old mill, classic white and brick Vermont houses, covered bridge, and waterfall, and turned it into a tasteful, elegant, and delightful place to enjoy visiting time and time again.

SIMON PEARCE

The Mill at Quechee
Quechee, VT 05059
(802) 295-1470
Open daily
9:00 a.m.–9:00 p.m.

VERMONT TRAVEL DIVISION

The fine art of glassblowing is practiced with skill at Simon Pearce in Quechee, Vermont.

"IF I HAD TIME FOR ONLY ONE LUNCH OR DINNER AT SIMON PEARCE I WOULD BE VERY UNHAPPY BECAUSE THERE ARE TOO MANY ITEMS I LOVE FOR A SINGLE MEAL."

—GOURMET, AUGUST 1989

One of our most fun evenings

Evening was? impromptu jives

Marvelous music

marvelous light food & people

Skunk Hollow Tavern

SKUNK HOLLOW TAVERN

Hartland 4 Corners
VT 05049
(802) 436-2139
Open daily at 5:30 p.m.
Closed Monday and Tuesday
Sunday brunch at 11:00 a.m.

FOR THE ADVENTUROUS, fun-loving gadabout, this is a place not to miss! It's a pub you have always looked for, no matter what country you are in; you open the door and are surrounded by atmosphere. There are eight or so tables in front of the wood fireplace in this cozy room with low beamed ceilings, wide-planked floors, period paintings, and people who have come to enjoy the conviviality. On the other side of the fireplace is the bar with its large comfortable bar stools and impressive view of bottles. You would not expect to find such an uncommonly fine selection of liquor, wine, and beer in a small pub.

Fish and chips, Hollow Burgers, and chicken Carlos are some of the delicious regulars on the menu, or you can choose among broiled swordfish, filet mignon, chicken enchiladas, and much more. The soups are outstanding; we had a salmon chowder that was exceptional along with a popover right out of the oven. Fresh garden salads are always available.

A delightful dining room upstairs for non-smokers shares the same menu and, although the atmosphere is the same, there is a little more elbow room.

On Sundays the door opens for brunch at 11 and closes after the last patron has finished dining. Wednesday night usually brings some sort of entertainment. This is a wonderful spot to "get away from it all" and have an unusually amusing evening. You can even take home a T-shirt as a souvenir.

Skunk Hollow is roughly in the middle of a triangle between Woodstock, White River Junction, and Windsor, no more than 20 or 25 minutes from any of these towns.

Stone Soup Restaurant

THERE ARE SEVERAL ROADS to Strafford, but it doesn't matter which one you take because the countryside on the way is the quintessence of Vermont scenery. The village common is small, neat, and appealing, and opposite the flag pole is Stone Soup, the only building on the common with a white picket fence in front. Don't bother looking for a sign, as there is none; all the advertising is word of mouth and that is all that's needed. You had better make a reservation before coming, and once here you'll find the food, character, mood, and people make dining at Stone Soup a memorable evening.

The two chef-owners, William Milne and Gil Robertson, bought this 1815 general store about ten years ago and totally renovated it to return both the interior and exterior to their original state. The town is on the National Register of Historic Places, and it's hard to believe you are in the 20th century when surrounded by such classic architectural splendor.

As you go through the front door you find yourself in the parlor, once the main room of the general store, a serene and inviting room with tasteful paintings, hand woven rugs, locally made furniture, and pottery, most of which is for sale. The beamed ceilings, wide board floors, and antiqued white walls, plus dried flowers all about, make your dining experience even more impressive.

The food is best described as home-cooked international fare. The portions are generous and the service is perfect. The entrées range from butterflied leg of lamb to the finest fish dishes imaginable.

Gil and William also take great pride in their prodigious herb and flower garden which, by the way, can be enjoyed while having dessert or drinks on the outside patio during the summer months. The abundance of flowers and fresh herbs is a treat that only adds to the pleasures of eating here.

STONE SOUP RESTAURANT

Strafford Common
P.O. Box 36
Strafford, VT 05072
(802) 765-4301

Open November to mid-June,
Thursday–Sunday,
6:00 p.m.–9:00 p.m.

Open mid-June
through October
Wednesday–Sunday,
6:00 p.m.–9:00 p.m.

❧

"SET AGAINST A SERENE BACKGROUND OF SLOPING GREEN FIELDS, THE RESTAURANT IS AS POPULAR FOR ITS INVITING ATMOSPHERE AS IT IS FOR ITS HEARTY CUSINE."

—COLONIAL HOMES,
JUNE 1991

A secret fishing hole along a trout stream somewhere in Vermont

VERMONT TRAVEL DIVISION

GAME & SEAFOOD

Chartreuse of Baby Pheasant
Pheasants à la Mode
Hasenpfeffer
Ivy Grill's Great Northern
    Bean & Game Chili
Wood-smoked Quail
Venison Chili
Autumn Venison
Venison Steaks with
    Black Pepper Sauce
Pan Roasted Scallops with
    Angel Hair Pasta & Red
    Pepper Vinaigrette
Sole Madras
Sautéed Scallops
    with Chutney
Shrimp Obregon à l'Absinthe
Kedron Valley Salmon
Fresh New England Sea
    Scallops with Basil Sauce
    & Red Bell Pepper Coulis
Grilled Swordfish
    with Garden Relish

Shrimp Royale
Scalloped Oysters
Broiled Halibut with
    Pistachio Lime Butter
Lobster with Champagne
Cajun Style
    Blackened Swordfish
Poached Fillet of Norwegian
    Salmon & Shrimp in a
    Saffron Broth with
    Potatoes & Spinach
Roulade of Sole with Smoked
    Salmon, Scallops,
    & Spinach Mousseline
Oriental Salmon
Sautéed Scallops with
    Papaya, Orange,
    & Chive Sauce
Mussels Marinara
Kentucky Bourbon Shrimp
    with Fresh Pasta
Shrimp Provençal

Chartreuse of Baby Pheasant

Remove the breast from the carcass keeping the first joint of the wing intact and leaving the skin of the breast covering the meat. Reserve for later.

Remove the leg leaving the leg bones in, then prepare a stock with the carcass, simmering three hours. Sauté the savoy and onion with the leg until all are lightly browned, deglaze with wine, and cover with stock. Braise for 45 minutes or until the meat comes from the bone easily. Layer into a buttered mold the braised meat, skin side down and in one piece. Salt and pepper the strained vegetables and then cover with at least ⅜-inch of a forcemeat of pork or veal (prepared by puréeing until smooth and being careful not to allow the mixture to become warm and using equal proportions of lean meat and heavy cream in a Cuisinart, plus salt and pepper, and a touch of fresh grated nutmeg).

Bake the mold for twenty minutes to set the forcemeat and let the skin brown slightly. Meanwhile reduce the braising liquid, add ½ cup of good wine and a tablespoon of whole grain mustard, reduce to be 4 ounces.

Sauté the breast, browning the skin, being sure not to overcook the meat, then salt and pepper. Invert the mold, cover the top of the Chartreuse with finely chopped parsley, plate the sauce, then the Chartreuse and finally the breast.

La Poule à Dents

SERVES 2

1 pound pheasant
½ carrot and ½ onion
1 tablespoon vinegar
1 quart water
1 cup savoy cabbage,
    juilienne
½ cup onion, juilienne
Whole grain mustard

⚜

THIS DISH CRIES OUT FOR GOOD BURGUNDY: VOLNAY-CAILLERETS, FIXIN, SANTENAY, MAZIS-CHAMBERTIN, ETC. OR AN OREGON RESERVE PINOT NOIR SUCH AS DOMAINE DROUHIN.

Pheasants à la Mode

SERVES 8

8 young pheasants
   (1½ pounds each)
Flour
¼ cup vegetable oil
2 shallots, coarsely
   chopped
1 cup chicken stock,
   or bouillon
½ cup dry white wine
1 anchovy fillet, as salt
Sweet herbs, such as
   marjoram, thyme,
   rosemary to taste
¼ teaspoon garlic
Parsley and red grape
   clusters

Cut each breast in half, keeping first wing joint attached. Remove leg, and keep only the thigh portion. Flour and brown in hot skillet or dutch oven. When quarters are well browned, add stock, wine , shallots, anchovy, and sweet herbs to taste. Cover tightly and simmer for about 30 minutes or until tender, turning periodically during cooking time. Remove pheasants to a hot platter. Skim fat and boil mixture briskly, stirring frequently until mixture is smooth.

Garnish birds with parsley and red grapes.

The Inn at Weathersfield

Hasenpfeffer

Marinate rabbit for two days in wine marinade. Keep refrigerated.

In a large Dutch oven, cook onions, mushrooms, and bacon until onions are soft. Lift out vegetables and bacon. Add 3 or 4 tablespoons butter to pan. Lift rabbit out of marinade; pat dry. Strain marinade. Sprinkle salt over rabbit; dip in flour; brown in butter. When all rabbit is brown, return with onion mixture to pan; pour strained marinade over rabbit and vegetables. Cover and simmer until tender, about one hour. Lift rabbit onto a heated platter. Stir salt and flour into sour cream; add to sauce in pan; spoon over rabbit.

The Lyme Inn

SERVES 8

2 rabbits, cut up (about 5 to 6 pounds) or chicken
1 recipe wine marinade (see below)
1½ cups diced onion
1 cup small or quartered mushrooms
4 slices bacon, cut up
3 to 4 tablespoons butter
2 teaspoons salt
½ cup all-purpose flour
½ cup sour cream

Wine Marinade:
2 cups wine
1 cup water
½ cup vinegar
1 tablespoon lemon juice
12 peppercorns
4 cloves garlic
½ teaspoon each thyme, rosemary, marjoram
1 cup celery leaves

Ivy Grill's Great Northern Bean & Game Chili

SERVES 8

8 to 12 ounces game
  meat
  (venison, moose,
  grilled or roasted
  pheasant, grouse,
  quail, or duck)
1 pound each Great
  Northern and pinto
  beans
½ cup each red, yellow,
  and green peppers,
  diced
3 cups diced onion
2 cups diced celery
3 bay leaves
8 "toes" crushed garlic
½ teaspoon chili
  powder
Fresh jalapeño, seeded,
  stemmed, and chopped

Salt and pepper to taste
1 tablespoon cocoa
  powder
1 teaspoon cumin
½ teaspoon coriander
½ teaspoon black
  pepper
½ bunch fresh cilantro,
  chopped
¼ bunch fresh thyme,
  leafed

Heat ¼ cup olive or peanut oil to light smoke. Add garlic and, immediately, onion. Add blanched beans (cook in salted water or with salt pork, vegetable or chicken stock for liquid).

Add seasonings and hot peppers to desired taste. Cook ½ to 1 hour until beans are tender.

Remove 2 cups beans and coarse purée and add back to give texture to chili. This is meatless chili at this point. If you desire you may add bacon or salt pork at beginning to get a desired flavor.

The meat garnish may be cooked in from the beginning like traditional chili or served along side or cooked at the last minute and placed around the serving dish. Garnish top with diced peppers.

Hanover Inn

IN PLACE OF JALAPEÑO, YOU CAN SUBSTITUTE SCOTCH BONNET, ANEHEIM OR SERRANIO, ALONE OR IN COMBINATION, TO SUIT YOUR TASTE. DRY SMOKED CHILIES ARE NICE IF YOU CAN FIND THEM.

ADRIAN N. BOUCHARD, 1975

*Frederick N. "Pete' Blodgett
Dartmouth '25*

Wood-smoked Quail

In small skillet, cook bacon until crisp; drain on paper towels; crumble. In a 10-inch skillet, heat olive oil over medium heat until it begins to smoke. Add onion and, while stirring, cook until translucent; do not brown. Add cabbage and bacon; cook and stir 3 minutes. Add butter, basil, rosemary, and nutmeg. Season to taste with salt and pepper; cook 2 minutes, stirring. Remove from heat; stir in goose liver. Cool completely.

Rinse cavities of quail with cold water; pat dry with paper towels. Spoon cooled stuffing into cavities. Tie legs together, and close cavities with toothpick.

Prepare smoker with wood chips according to manufacturer's directions. Without crowding, smoke stuffed quail over very low heat for 8 minutes. Refrigerate.

To make sauce, heat chicken broth to boiling in large saucepan. Stirring occasionally, boil until reduced to 2 cups. In small saucepan over medium heat, combine port and Madeira; boil until reduced to about 2 tablespoons. Stir wines into chicken broth.

Remove quail from refrigerator about 40 minutes before serving; let stand at room temperature.

Preheat oven to 450°F. Reheat sauce. Roast quail on rack in open roasting pan 5 minutes. Spoon ¼ cup sauce onto each plate. Arrange quail in sauce.

Hemingway's

SERVES 8

8 deboned quail
2 strips bacon
2 tablespoons olive oil
1 small onion, thinly sliced
4 cups finely shredded green cabbage
¼ cup (½ stick) butter
1 teaspoon basil
1 teaspoon rosemary, crushed
½ teaspoon nutmeg
Salt and pepper
2 tablespoons puréed goose liver
Smoker or covered barbecue grill prepared for smoking
Alder wood chips or other wood chips for smoker
8 cups unsalted chicken broth
½ cup port
½ cup Madeira

Venison Chili

SERVES 8 TO 10

1 pound ground venison
(Uncle Buck's)
1 pound cubed venison
(Uncle Buck's)
2 tablespoons olive oil
4 finely chopped medium
onions
3 cloves crushed garlic
3 fresh tomatoes, cut up
4 tablespoons tomato
paste
1 bay leaf
1 each green and red bell
peppers, chopped
1 teaspoon each ground
cumin, oregano,
and chili powder

¼ teaspoon cayenne
pepper
1½ teaspoons herbal salt
substitute
1 cup beef stock
2 tablespoons brown
sugar
2 small cans mild green
chili peppers, chopped
28-ounce can red kidney
beans

Heat oil in large heavy saucepan. Sauté onions, garlic, and bell peppers until soft, but not browned. Brown meat separately and add to vegetables. Stir in tomatoes, tomato paste, seasonings, stock, and bring to a boil.

Reduce to low, add chili peppers, and cover. Simmer for two hours, stirring occasionally. Stir in kidney beans and simmer for 3 minutes more.

Remove bay leaf and serve with rice or noodles, with green salad, and fresh baked sour dough or French bread.

Gourmet Garden

Autumn Venison

SERVES 2

4 two-ounce medallions
of venison, loin cut
1 ounce clarified butter
Flour for dredging
6 medium morel
mushrooms
¼ cup roasted shelled
chestnuts
2 ounces marsala wine
3 ounces veal demi-glace

Heat butter in a sauté pan. Dredge venison medallions in flour. Cook for 2 minutes each side. Add morel mushrooms and chestnuts, heat for 1 minute, then add marsala wine. Be sure to flame off alcohol. When flame goes out add demi-glace. Remove venison, reduce sauce, and lay over venison.

The Inn at Norwich

Venison Steaks with Black Pepper Sauce

With sharp boning knife, cut two fillets from venison saddle. Trim off silvery membrane and sinews; reserve bones and trimmings. Cut fillets into 6 to 8 serving pieces; cover, and refrigerate.

To make sauce base, preheat oven to 450°F. Chop saddle bone into small pieces. Place bones and trimmings in open roasting pan. Roast 30 minutes or until bones are well browned. Add vegetables, garlic, and bouquet garni. Roast 5 minutes. Sprinkle flour over mixture; stir gently to combine. Roast 10 minutes. Transfer bones and vegetables to 4- or 5-quart saucepan; set aside.

Add cognac and ½ cup vinegar to roasting pan; cook over medium heat, stirring to loosen browned bits. Pour cognac mixture over bones; add red wine and peppercorns, and heat to boiling. Reduce heat, cover, and simmer 2 hours.

Strain liquid from saucepan through fine mesh sieve, pressing vegetables and bones to extract as much liquid as possible. Reserve 1½ cups sauce base for sauce below. Pour remaining sauce base into 1- or 2-cup freezer-safe containers. Freeze to use as base for other sauces and gravies.

Sprinkle venison steaks with salt and pepper. Heat olive oil in large heavy-gauge skillet over medium-high heat. Add steaks; brown well on each side, keeping center of meat pink. Remove steaks, and keep warm.

Spoon excess fat from skillet. Add remaining 2 tablespoons vinegar; cook, stirring to loosen browned bits. Add reserved 1½ cups sauce base; heat to boiling while stirring. Remove from heat; whisk in butter. Correct seasoning. Serve sauce over steaks.

Hemingway's

SERVES 6 TO 8

1 seven-pound bone-in saddle of venison (full length of fillet)
2 onions, diced
2 carrots, diced
2 ribs celery, diced
8 shallots, diced
8 mushrooms, sliced
4 cloves garlic, crushed
1 bouquet garni (parsley, thyme, and bay leaf)
1 cup all purpose flour
¼ cup cognac
½ cup plus 2 tablespoons red wine vinegar
2 liters red wine
2 teaspoons peppercorns, crushed
Salt and pepper
2 teaspoons olive oil
1 tablespoon butter

Pan Roasted Scallops with Angel Hair Pasta & Red Pepper Vinaigrette

SERVES 4

1 red pepper, charred on
    open flame and peeled
1 teaspoon salt
1 teaspoon freshly cracked
    black pepper
¼ cup red wine vinegar
½ cup peanut oil
¼ cup olive oil
¼ cup heavy cream
1 pound large sea scallops

Combine all ingredients except scallops in a saucepot. Bring to a simmer then blend in a blender.

Cut scallops the same thickness and remove white muscle on the side. Using a teflon pan, lightly oil scallops and place them in the pan. Cook for 30 seconds on each side. Pour the sauce on a plate. Place pasta in the middle then arrange scallops around the pasta. Serve immediately.

New England Culinary Institute

Sole Madras

Curry Powder:
4 tablespoon coriander
3 tablespoons cumin
3 tablespoons turmeric
3 tablespoons cardamom
1 teaspoon mace
1 teaspoon cinnamon
1 teaspoon cloves
½ teaspoon cayenne

Relish:
1 medium tomato and
    ½ cucumber
¼ medium onion, all
    chunked
Add 1 tablespoon
    vinegar and salt to
    taste
1 tablespoon chopped
    parley

Grind finely all the ingredients; put in glass jar and shake well. Mix ⅓ curry powder and ⅔ flour. Season sole fillets with salt and lemon juice. Let marinade for 10 to 15 minutes. Dry lightly, then dip in flour curry mix in large skillet with thin layer of sesame seed oil. Heat to almost smoking. Lay in fish and ½ banana, which you first dip in the curry flour mix also. Brown, turn, and brown. Arrange on plate. Brown a teaspoon of chopped almonds, then add freshly chopped pineapple. Sauté until all juice is reduced. Add a tablespoon of lemon juice and a teaspoon of chopped parsley or cilantro. Put topping on fish and decorate with fresh fruit such as mango, papaya, kiwis, peaches, or berries. Serve with mango chutney and fresh cucumber or tomato.

Barnard Inn

Shrimp Obregon a l'Absinthe

Sauté shrimps with the lemon and garlic in butter. Salt and pepper to taste. When done (do not overcook), remove shrimps from pan, discard lemon zest and garlic. Reduce shrimp juice until pan is almost dry, add cream and Pernod and cook until the sauce is reduced to half. To finish, put shrimps back in same pan with the sauce. Shake well and serve.

The Woodstock Inn & Resort

1 pound shrimps
  (cleaned, peeled and
  deveined)
2 whole peeled garlic
  cloves
2 thin zests of lemon skin
1 cup heavy cream
  (whipping cream)
1 ounce butter
1 to 2 ounces Pernod
Optional additions:
Vermont cheddar cheese
Wild mushrooms
Leeks
Galliano
Fresh herbs

Sautéed Scallops with Chutney

Mix together the first 6 ingredients and cook over low heat for approximately 1 hour.

Cook the butter, scallops, and white wine at high heat for approximately 1 minute. Then add the chutney and mustard and continue cooking until the scallops are done. Garnish with lemon wedge and parsley.

Mountain Top Inn and Resort

SERVES 1

1 cup bay scallops
1 chopped tomato
1 seeded, cored apple
¼ cup raisins
¼ cup brown sugar
1 teaspoon allspice
1 teaspoon curry
1 teaspoon butter
2 tablespoons white wine
½ teaspoon Dijon
  mustard
1 tablespoon chutney

Grilled Swordfish with Garden Relish

SERVES 2

2 six-ounce swordfish
   steaks

Swordfish marinade:
1 tablespoon canola oil
1 tablespoon fresh
   chopped basil
1 teaspoon minced garlic
Dash salt and pepper

Garden Relish:
1 cucumber, peeled,
   seeded, diced, and set
   aside in a bowl
½ red bell pepper, diced
½ yellow bell pepper,
   diced
1 scallion, diced

1 teaspoon minced garlic
Zest of ½ lemon
Juice of ¼ lemon
3 tablespoons fresh,
   chopped basil
1 tablespoon chopped
   parsley
1 teaspoon extra virgin
   olive oil

Combine oil, herbs, and seasonings in a glass bowl. Put swordfish in the bowl and marinate for half an hour.

Combine all the relish ingredients except for the cucumber. Heat 2 teaspoons canola oil in a skillet until very hot. Sauté the combined vegetables in the oil for about 10 to 15 seconds, tossing constantly until slightly softened. Add the mixed vegetables to the cucumbers. Then add remaining ingredients, stir, and pour the relish into a pitcher.

Relish may sit at room temperature while you grill the swordfish. Approximate grilling time: 4 to 5 minutes per side.

Quechee Inn at Marshland Farm

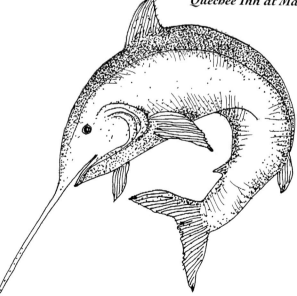

Shrimp Royale

Peel and devein shrimps, leaving on tail. Slice down back ¾ through and set aside. Put crabmeat, blue cheese, and garlic in mixer and blend well. Add salt and pepper to taste. Stuff shrimps and place on buttered casserole dish. Bake at 400°F until shrimps are cooked, about 15 minutes.

While shrimps are cooking, make sauce. In a sauté pan, melt butter and add shallots. Cook until soft. Add wine and reduce by half. Add heavy cream, salt, and pepper. Reduce by half. Spoon over cooked shrimps.

The Inn at Norwich

SERVES 4

12 large shrimps
1 cup crabmeat
6 ounces blue cheese
2 teaspoons chopped
 garlic
Salt and pepper to taste

Sauce:
1 ounce butter
3 ounces champagne
½ teaspoon chopped
 shallots
1 cup heavy cream
1 pinch each of salt and
 pepper

Scalloped Oysters

Brush 2-quart casserole with butter. Cover bottom with crackers and dot with about 6 or 8 nut-size fresh butter pieces. Layer with oysters, salt and pepper, and pinch of winter savory. Repeat, and continue until top layer, then top with crackers and butter. Top with cream, shake casserole to distribute cream.

Bake at 375°F until edges bubble and top browns, 15 to 20 minutes. Serve immediately.

Hanover Inn

SERVES 8 TO 10

1 quart shucked oysters
1 stick butter
15 to 20 common
 crackers, cracked in
 ½" pieces
 (or 2 cups Bremner
 wafers or saltines)
Winter savory
Salt and pepper
1 pint cream

Broiled Halibut
with Pistachio Lime Butter

SERVES 4

4 six-ounce halibut
    fillets
2 tablespoons olive oil
¾ cup dry white wine
1 tablespoon chopped
    shallots
1 tablespoon heavy cream
10 ounces unsalted butter
2 limes
½ cup toasted, chopped
    pistachio nuts
2 cups chopped romaine
    lettuce

Rub halibut with olive oil, salt, and pepper and place on broiler rack. Sprinkle with ¼ cup white wine. Combine ½ cup white wine with shallots in non-aluminum pan and reduce by half. Add heavy cream and juice of 1 lime.

To make the sauce, whip in 8 ounces very cold butter cut into small pieces, one piece at a time, over medium heat. Strain and keep warm. Start fish cooking. Melt remaining 2 ounces butter over medium high heat and sauté romaine very quickly (do not overcook). Divide romaine and butter sauce among 4 plates: sprinkle with nuts. Set broiled fish atop and garnish with remaining lime, peeled and cut into dice.

Quechee Inn at Marshland Farm

Lobster with Champagne

Preheat oven to 450°F. Place lobsters in large roasting pan; brush with oil. Roast 15 to 20 minutes. Remove from oven, and cool.

To make sauce, combine champagne, shallots, saffron, and thyme in small saucepan. Boil until liquid is reduced to about 2 tablespoons. Over very low heat, add butter, 2 tablespoons at a time, whisking after each addition until thickened. Stir in cream, lemon juice, and salt. Pour into serving dish; let stand at room temperature.

Twist off lobster claws at body section. Remove meat from claws; set aside. Place each lobster on its back. With poultry shears or sharp knife, split lobsters open. Remove inedible parts from body cavity, and replace with claw meat. Ladle warm sauce over meat. Serve over corn.

Hemingway's

SERVES 4

4 one-and-a-quarter to one-and-a-half pound lobsters
¼ cup olive oil
1 cup champagne or dry white wine
2 large shallots, chopped
Pinch saffron
Pinch thyme leaves
1 cup butter, softened
2 tablespoons heavy or whipping cream
2 tablespoons lemon juice
⅛ teaspoon salt
Fresh corn, cooked

Cajun Style Blackened Swordfish

SERVES 6

6 fresh swordfish steaks
2 sweet peppers of
various colors
1 onion
10 mushrooms
Seasoning mix
Lemon juice
Melted butter

Slice sweet pepper into strips. Do the same with an onion and slice mushrooms.

You can make your own season-blackening mix, but you're better off with the excellent pre-mixed product that Chef Paul Prudhomme makes and sells in the local grocery.

Use fresh swordfish steaks, preferably with no belly strip, about 1½ inches thick. Coat the fish first with lemon juice, then dunk in melted butter. Put seasoning on a flat plate and completely coat both sides of fish by pressing into seasoning.

Put a good black cast-iron skillet or thick aluminum skillet on the stove or burner on high heat for about 10 to 15 minutes. It can't be too hot. Use a pot holder or towel to handle it. Put the coated swordfish into the pan and press down with a spatula. It's really going to get smoky! Turn fish over when you see the juices start to come through to the surface of the steak. Cook until done. Check by cutting open if you have to. Be careful not to dry it out. Both sides should be black.

⚜

UNLESS YOU HAVE REALLY GOOD VENTILATION IN YOUR KITCHEN, DON'T TRY THIS INSIDE. INSTEAD USE A GOOD GAS BURNER OUTSIDE.

While your fish is cooking, put 2 ounces of butter in a pan with half of the sweet pepper mix. Add a dash of leftover seasoning and cook until peppers are soft, then add the rest of the veggies and cook until just crisp. By this time the first part of the mix should be almost caramelized. Top the swordfish with this and dream about Louisiana while savoring every bite.

Lake Sunapee Country Club

Poached Fillet of Norwegian Salmon & Shrimp in a Saffron Broth with Potatoes & Spinach

Bone the salmon and reserve the fillet. Slice the fillet into ½-inch steaks weighing 3 to 4 ounces. Prepare a stock with the bones and leek tops, and let simmer 45 minutes. Strain the bones and poach the potatoes, carrots, and onions in the stock until tender.

Add the saffron and let stock sit 5 minutes to infuse the saffron. Place the spinach in a mound in the center of a 10-inch sauté pan on top of the poached vegetables and 1 cup of the fish stock. Surround the spinach with the shrimp, peppers, and shiitake mushrooms, and lay the fillets on top of the spinach, then salt and pepper.

Cover and heat until the salmon is cooked through. It will not take long so do not leave it alone. At the last second add a tablespoon of heavy cream and gently swirl the sauce around the pan to allow it to blend uniformly. Serve immediately on warm plate, arranging the fillet in the center on top of the spinach, surrounded by the shrimp and vegetables in a pool of broth.

La Poule à Dents

SERVES 12

6-pound Norwegian salmon
60 peeled medium shrimps
Leek tops

4 medium potatoes diced into ⅓-inch dice
2 medium onions, diced
2 pounds washed and stemmed spinach
1 red pepper, julienne
3 carrots, ⅓-inch dice
½ pound shiitake mushrooms
Pinch of saffron
½ cup heavy cream

Roulade of Sole with Smoked Salmon, Scallops, & Spinach Mousseline

SERVES 4

1¼ pound sole fillets
¼ pound scallops
2 ounces smoked salmon
½ cup heavy cream
1 tablespoon cognac
½ pound spinach,
     washed and blanched
Salt and white pepper, to
     taste

To make the mousseline: Keep as cold as possible while making. In a food processor purée the scallops and smoked salmon, add the cognac and process again. Transfer to a bowl and put that bowl in another bowl with ice and water to keep it well chilled. Slowly add the cream, beating with a spoon. You may not need all the cream; add as much as possible while still having it hold its shape. Season with salt and pepper.

To make roulades: Lay 4 sole fillets on a large piece of plastic wrap, then lay another piece of plastic wrap on top. With the side of a large chef's knife lightly flatten the fillets. Remove top layer of plastic wrap and lay the blanched spinach leaves in a single layer on top of the sole. Spread an even layer of the mousseline over the surface of each fillet.

Roll sole, starting at one end and rolling to the other end. Roll each sole in a piece of plastic and twist the ends to secure; it should look like a sausage. Twist the sole while holding each end; this will tighten the sole and secure the ends. Repeat with remaining fillets. Refrigerate until ready to poach.

To poach the fish: In a large pot of simmering water place the sole roulades and simmer gently for 12 minutes. Remove from the water and let rest 5 minutes. Unwrap and slice, then place on plates.

To make the sauce: In a small sauté pan put 1 tablespoon of butter and heat over medium heat. Add the shallots and cook for 1 minute. Add ¼ cup white wine, reduce to 2 tablespoons, then add 2 tablespoons cream and reduce slightly. Whisk in 8 tablespoons of unsalted butter until just incorporated. Season to taste with lemon juice and pepper. If you want, add 2 table-spoons chopped fresh herb of your choice. Serve immediately over the sole.

Sauce Beurre Blanc:
9 tablespoons butter
2 tablespoons finely chopped shallots
¼ cup white wine
2 tablespoons cream
Juice of ½ lemon
2 tablespoons chopped herbs, such as dill or basil (optional)

Café La Fraise

Oriental Salmon

SERVES 4

About 1½ pounds
   salmon fillet
6 tablespoons dark
   roasted sesame oil
2 ribs celery, thinly sliced
1 sweet red pepper, cut in
   julienne strips
1 yellow pepper, cut in
   julienne strips
4 scallions (white part
   only), sliced
2 tablespoons diced fresh
   gingerroot
1 head (about 1 pound)
   bok choy, thinly sliced
2 tablespoons soy sauce
1 cup chicken broth
Juice of 1 orange (½ cup)
¼ cup Hoisin sauce
1 tablespoon diced garlic
1 star anise or 1 teaspoon
   anise seed
1 teaspoon wild
   mushroom powder or
   ½ cup sliced fresh
   mushrooms
1 tablespoon arrowroot
   or 2 tablespoons
   cornstarch
1 tablespoon water
¼ cup olive oil
Wild rice (optional)
Green onion tops
   (optional)

With large sharp knife, trim skin from salmon fillet; scrape off any dark flesh. Cut salmon into 1½-inch pieces; set aside.

In a 10-inch skillet over medium-high flame, heat 2 tablespoons sesame oil. Add celery, peppers, scallions, and 1 tablespoon gingerroot. Cook 2 minutes, stirring quickly. Add bok choy and 1 tablespoon soy sauce. Cook 2 minutes longer, stirring; set aside.

In small saucepan, combine remaining sesame oil, gingerroot, and soy sauce with chicken broth, orange juice, Hoisin sauce, garlic, anise, and mushroom powder. Heat to boiling while stirring; simmer 10 minutes. Dissolve arrowroot in cold water; stir into saucepan. Boil 1 minute, stirring constantly. Pour sauce mixture through fine sieve over vegetables. Toss to combine; keep warm.

In large skillet over medium-high flame, heat olive oil to sizzling. Add salmon; cook until crisp and brown on both sides and medium-rare in center. Place vegetables on large platter; top with salmon. Serve with wild rice and chopped green onion tops.

Hemingway's

JERRY LEBLOND

The views from Mountain Top Inn are spectacular in all seasons

TULIP TREE INN

Quiet seclusion in a beautiful setting makes the Tulip Tree Inn a special place for vacationers

JERRY LEBLOND

JERRY LEBLOND

This 1860 stagecoach stop is now the home of Hemingway's,
the only four-star, four-diamond restaurant in northern New England.

JERRY LEBLOND

The more formal dining room at Hemingway's features a lovely collection of work by
local artists.

On a clear day the scenery from Killington's gondala is spectacular

The Cortina Inn is close to the base of Pico Peak

Sautéed Scallops with a Papaya, Orange, & Chive Sauce

Clean the scallops, then soak in milk. When ready to use, drain and dry on paper towels.

Heat 2 tablespoons butter and 1 tablespoon oil in a sauté pan until butter stops foaming, and add scallops. Sauté scallops for 3 to 4 minutes; do not overcook. Remove from pan. Add the shallots to the pan and cook for 1 minute; add wine and reduce until slightly thickened. Add the papaya purée, orange juice, and orange segments, bring to a boil and let simmer for 2 minutes.

Add the pieces of butter to pan, whisking constantly until butter is just incorporated. Do not overheat or the sauce will separate. Add chives and taste for seasoning.

Place cooked scallops on plates and pour sauce over them.

Café La Fraise

SERVES 2

¾ pound scallops
1 papaya, puréed
1 orange, cut into segments (save any juice)
½ cup white wine
1 shallot
1 ounce unsalted butter
1 teaspoon chopped chives

Mussels Marinara

SERVES 4 TO 6

60 mussels, cleaned and
    bearded
4 large peeled, deveined
    raw shrimp
½ cup white wine
2 cups chopped tomatoes
1 tablespoon tomato
    paste
½ medium onion

1 stalk celery
4 cloves garlic
½ teaspoon basil
½ teaspoon thyme
½ teaspoon parsley
Salt
Black pepper
½ lemon

Sauté onion, celery, and garlic until soft. Add to tomato and tomato paste. Add tomato mixture to wine and heat. Combine mussels, shrimp, and juice of lemon. Cook covered over medium heat, stirring often until mussels are open, 5 to 7 minutes.

Serve with French bread.

Kedron Valley Inn

Kentucky Bourbon Shrimp with Fresh Pasta

Sauté the shrimps for a minute with the first 7 ingredients at highest temperature. Carefully pour in the bourbon. Do not pour direct from glass bottle; it can explode. Let flame and add the marinara to extinguish the bourbon. Add the dill and simmer until vegetables are al dente.

Serve over pasta, the thinner the pasta the better. Orzo is a good variation too.

Powderhounds

⚜

THE SECRET TO THIS DISH IS TWOFOLD. FIRST, PREPARATION AND SPEED; SECOND, NOT ALLOWING ALL THE ALCOHOL TO EVAPORATE WHEN YOU FLAMBÉ THE SHRIMP.

PER SERVING:

6 to 7 ounces fresh peeled and deveined shrimps, the larger the better
1 tablespoon olive oil
1 teaspoon fresh garlic, minced
1 tablespoon fresh shallots, minced
1 tablespoon fresh leek (white only), julienne
1 tablespoon red onion, julienne
5 to 6 pieces sun-dried tomatoes
2 to 3 ounces Kentucky bourbon
Thin marinara sauce
Fresh dill
Fresh pasta (angel hair or vermicelli are best)

Shrimp Provençal

SERVES 6 TO 8

2 pounds of shrimps,
    peeled and deveined,
    any size you prefer
1 to 1½ pounds of boxed
or frozen linguini or
    fettucine, cooked
    al dente, rinsed,
    oiled, and cooled

Provencal Mix:
¼ cup capers
½ cup chopped black
    olives
½ cup chopped celery
½ cup chopped scallions
½ cup chopped green
    peppers

2½ cups chopped, seeded
    tomatoes
2 tablespoons fresh
    chopped garlic
1 tablespoon oregano
½ tablespoon basil
½ tablespoon parsley
2 tablespoons lemon juice
½ cup white wine
1 cup tomato juice
1 teaspoon salt
    or 1 tablespoon
    of clam base
½ teaspoon of black
    pepper

Combine all ingredients
except shrimps and pasta
in a stainless steel bowl.

Using a 14- to 16-inch sauté pan, put in 2 tablespoons of olive oil and enough shrimps for 1 or 2 portions. Cook shrimps half-way and add 1 or 2 cups of Provençal mix. Cook until shrimps and veggies are done, but do not evaporate all the liquid.

Mix in whatever pasta is necessary for the portions and heat through, stirring constantly. Put on plates and serve with fresh grated Parmesan or Romano cheese and garlic French bread.

Lake Sunapee Country Club

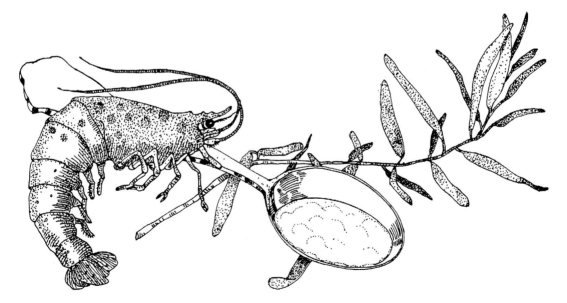

KILLINGTON

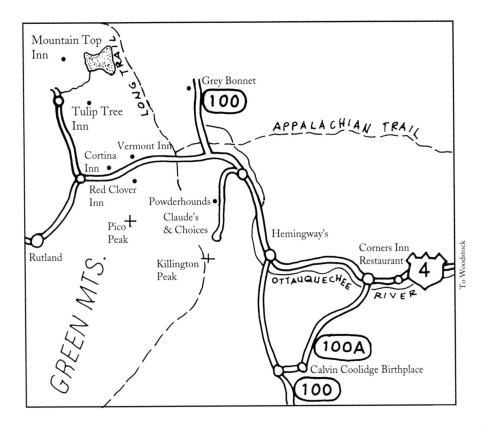

Mountain Top
Inn

LONG TRAIL

Grey Bonnet
100

APPALACHIAN TRAIL

Tulip Tree
Inn

Vermont Inn

Cortina
Inn

Red Clover
Inn

Powderhounds ●

Claude's
& Choices

Hemingway's

Corners Inn
Restaurant

To Woodstock

Pico +
Peak

Rutland

Killington +
Peak

GREEN MTS.

OTTAUQUECHEE

RIVER

4

100A

Calvin Coolidge Birthplace

100

Killington, Vermont

*A*lthough Killington is widely known as New England's largest ski resort, it is also becoming one of the most extensive all-season destination resorts in the East. There is a lot going on in Killington all the time, and it's easy to have fun here in the summer as well as winter or whenever you visit.

In warm weather, for example, to spice its traditional Vermont attractions of lovely inns and fine restaurants, Killington has a wonderful music festival as well as many other musical events such as jazz and bluegrass, band concerts, and children's programs, plus the Hartford Ballet, road races, and even a circus. There is an excellent School for Tennis featuring two-day weekends or five-day midweek sessions that use the Accelerated Teaching Method. The Geoffrey Cornish-designed PGA golf course in Killington Village is a great test of golf on a beautiful layout, and tee times are available to visitors.

As for Killington's justly famous skiing, its six interconnected peaks and ten separate ski areas quite literally comprise a ski area of superlatives. It has 18 lifts and more than 77 miles of trails for every level of skier. Killington has the most extensive snow-making system in the world, the longest ski trail and longest lift in America, and the steepest slope and longest vertical drop in New England.

Most of this was only a dream when Preston Leete Smith, an enthusiastic young skier and fledgling ski developer, opened Killington in December, 1958, with four lifts and seven trails. And while other ski areas relegated novice snowbirds to slopes at lower elevations, Smith built beginner trails from each summit, encouraging new skiers to greater heights right away. It was a smash from the start, and Killington has never stopped growing and improving since.

A TRIP UP KILLINGTON PEAK IN THE KILLINGTON CHAIRLIFT IS A MARVELOUS FAMILY EXCURSION. SITUATED AT THE TOP OF THE ACCESS ROAD, THIS 1¼ MILE CHAIRLIFT WILL TAKE YOU TO THE RESTAURANT, OBSERVATION DECK, AND SELF-GUIDED NATURE TRAIL TO THE SUMMIT CONE, WHERE IN 1763 THE STATE WAS CHRISTENED "VERD-MONT."

In another precedent-setting innovation, Killington installed snow-making equipment for the 1962-63 season. Other ski operators shook their heads in derision, but the move proved fortuitous when the following year most of the doubters were forced to close by lack of snow. Later Killington, collaborating with Ski Magazine, introduced a revolutionary teaching system called the Graduated Length Method, and followed that up by pioneering the all-inclusive "Ski Week."

Killington wasn't always so imposing. First settled in 1790 by 32 hardy souls, the town's population grew to a peak in 1850 of 578 people and 1,450 sheep. At that time logging, wool production, and stoneworking were the primary sources of income. But then, as now, environmental concerns became important, and the combined effect of overhunting, overfarming, and excessive logging brought a drop in the number of residents as ambitious young men went West for greater opportunities.

Then the rairoads arrived, bringing with them tourists to fill the void. Rustic mountain hotels began to dominate the area, even though in the 1800s some of them located near the Killington Mountain summit were reachable only by miles-long dirt roads. But they too faded with time, and eventually the Vermont Marble Company bought thousands of acres of Killington lands, established another prosperous logging operation, and in 1945 sold the land to the state for about $7 an acre.

Then along came Preston Smith, and Killington was never the same. Today there are many attractive places for visitors to stay, and a number of fine restaurants serving fabulous food. All in all, it's always a wonderful place for either a quick visit or a more leisurely vacation.

⚜

PICO PEAK, NEXT DOOR TO KILLINGTON BUT NOT YET PART OF THE KILLINGTON COMPLEX, IS ANOTHER FABULOUS PLACE TO SKI AND IS NOT AS LARGE OR BUSY AS KILLINGTON. IT HAS TWO HIGH-SPEED QUADS SERVICING THE 4,000-FOOT SUMMIT, AND NEARLY 2,000 FEET OF VERTICAL DROP. THE PICO ALPINE SLIDE IS ONE OF THE MOST THRILLING SUMMER ATTRACTIONS IN THE GADABOUTS AREA. YOU BOARD THE TRIPLE CHAIRLIFT AND RIDE TO THE TOP, WHERE YOU CLIMB ONTO THE ALPINE SLIDE FOR A BREATHTAK-ING 3,400-FOOT RIDE TO THE BOTTOM.

Cortina Inn

CORTINA INN

Route 4
Killington, VT 05751
Tel. (802) 773-3331
(800) 451-6108
Fax (802) 775-6948
Open year-round

✤

"THE WARM HOSPITALITY
OF BOB AND BREDA
HARNISH MADE ME FORGET
THE TWO FEET
OF SNOW OUTSIDE."
—WOMAN'S DAY

✤

"THE CORTINA INN, A
COMPLETE RESORT KNOWN
FOR ITS EXCELLENT FOOD"
—GLAMOUR

✤

"BEST PLACE TO STAY WHEN
SKIING NORTHERN NEW
ENGLAND"
—SKIING MAGAZINE

CORTINA INN, ONE OF VERMONT'S loveliest four-season destination resorts, is located in a beautiful valley only minutes from the Killington and Pico ski areas. Whether spring, summer, fall, or winter, virtually everything you could want is within a few steps of your door. The owners and innkeepers, Bob and Breda Harnish, have created a most attractive place to relax and enjoy the perfect "Vermont getaway."

Renowned for offering guests the charming hospitality of a country inn with the splendid amenities of a full service resort hotel, Cortina Inn has 98 individually decorated rooms, with the emphasis on personal comfort. In some of the deluxe rooms and suites you can warm yourself by a fireplace or enjoy the surrounding scenery from your balcony or terrace.

The Inn recently entered into an agreement with the world-famous New England Culinary Institute to manage its kitchens under the supervision of Executive Chef Robert Barral and Chef Instructor George Carone. The Harnishes are particularly pleased with the NECI touch to the food at Cortina Inn, and the response from diners has been overwhelmingly positive. The food served in the handsome Oak Room is unparalleled, with so many daily specials it's impossible to list them all. This room is especially comfortable with attractively appointed full-size tables and armchairs for everyone. The ideal place to end your evening at the inn is Theodore's Lounge, a comfortable and inviting downstairs bar featuring nighttime musical entertainment.

On-site features include a fully equipped tennis center with eight courts and professional instruction, a health spa with indoor pools, hot tub and saunas, a library and game room, and an art gallery featuring paintings and sculptures by local artisans. Skating, sleigh rides, and snowmobiling are "on campus" activities for all ages.

New England Culinary Institute

ALTHOUGH New England Culinary Institute (NECI) is in Montpelier and Essex, Vermont, a bit outside the territory covered in this book, it would be a serious omission if we did not tell you about this extraordinary cooking school. Since there are so many interning and graduate chefs of the Institute working in the *Gadabouts* area, and now that NECI is managing the kitchens at the Cortina Inn in Killington, we felt we would be cheating our readers if we did not tell you something about the school or include some of their recipes in this book.

New England Culinary Institute was founded in 1980 by Francis Voigt and John Dranow, both former educators at Goddard College in Plainfield. The first class was made up of eight students. In 1992, over 400 students are enrolled, and they come from all 50 states and from 15 foreign countries. Although the average age is 24, there are students 18 to 55 years old, and the student-teacher ratio is never more than 7 to 1. The credentials of the key personnel, instructional and administrative, are impeccable; their backgrounds are professional and particularly well suited to their positions at NECI.

The students spend 75 percent of their time in a hands-on environment, cooking and managing the school's many different food services that are open to the public. They spend two of their four semesters in a paid internship program, where they work in any type of food service anywhere in the United States and abroad that meets the school's standards. All of the graduates are placed in the culinary field, with the average graduate receiving five or six job offers.

Many of NECI's graduates are becoming famous nationally and internationally. The more you visit restaurants where NECI interns and graduates are cooking, the more you will be impressed with their skill and imagination in preparing unforgettable meals.

NEW ENGLAND CULINARY INSTITUTE

250 Main Street
RR#1 Box 1255
Montpelier, VT 05620
Tel. (802) 223-6324
Fax (802) 223-0634

⚜

WE HAVE WORKED PROFESSIONALLY WITH SEVERAL STUDENTS FROM THE NEW ENGLAND CULINARY INSTITUTE AND HAVE BEEN DELIGHTED WITH THEIR WORK AND ESPECIALLY WITH THEIR ATTITUDES AND MOTIVATION.
—JULIA CHILD, CHEF AND AUTHOR.

Claude's and Choices Restaurants

CLAUDE'S AND CHOICES

Glazebrook Center
Killington Road
Killington, VT 05751
(802) 422-4030

Claude's is open every day in winter and Thursday–Sunday other seasons. Hours: 6:00 p.m.–10:00 p.m.

Choices is open every day in winter and Wednesday–Sunday other seasons. Hours: 5:00 p.m.–10:00 p.m.

⚜

"YOU'RE ABOUT TO HAVE THE BEST FOOD YOU'VE EVER EATEN...NO IFS, ANDS, OR BUTS ABOUT THAT!"
—RUTLAND DAILY HERALD, FEBRUARY 1991

CLAUDE BLAIS, THE CHEF-OWNER of these two restaurants (in one building) has put together two types of fine dining experience for visitors to the Killington area.

Claude's emphasizes Continental food and is the more formal of the pair. It has a particularly handsome dining room featuring attractive modern art from local artists, large comfortable burgundy chairs, white linen, classic tableware, soft lights and music, and other tasteful amenities that help make an evening here one to remember. The classic menu changes often and includes something for everyone. The rack of lamb is famous and the fresh seafood dishes are outstanding. The wine list is impressive. By the time you finish one of this talented chef's entrees and think you couldn't eat another thing, think again, because the desserts are not to be forgotten.

Choices is on the front side of the building facing the Killington ski slopes. The dining room, with an impressive bar, is brighter and more casual than Claude's with somewhat livelier music. Although the menu reflects the more informal atmosphere, the food is excellent and presented beautifully. Choices is billed as a "Chef Owned Restaurant–Bistro–American Cafe–Pub" and it really is all of these. Choices also offers a Sunday brunch that is famous and worth a visit.

Grey Bonnet Inn

THE GREY BONNET INN, surrounded by dense pine woods and spectacular views, is an unusually comfortable country inn built in 1972. Of the 42 pleasant bedrooms, some have king-size beds, while others have two doubles or one queen. All have an individual thermostat, private bath, color TV, air conditioning and telephone. Most of the rooms have small private decks for enjoying the lovely scenery.

Recreation of all sorts is also available at the Grey Bonnet. There is a wonderful all-weather tennis court in the woods and both indoor and outdoor swimming pools. Spa facilities include an exercise room, a Finnish sauna, a whirlpool, and a tanning room. Just around the corner is the well-known Mountain Meadows Cross-Country Ski Touring Center, whose trails connect with those of the Grey Bonnet. Equipment rentals, maps, and instruction are all available at the Touring Center.

The Innkeepers, Bill and Barbara Flohr, have good reason to be proud of their award-winning chef, Rex Doperak, who prepares mouth-watering meals in the newly renovated dining room. The menu changes with the seasons, offering a number of different entrées each evening, from fresh pasta and seafood to specially prepared duck and veal dishes. There is a piano player in the dining room Thursday, Friday, and Saturday to make the evening meal even more enjoyable.

GREY BONNET INN

Route 100 North
Killington, VT 05751
(802) 775-2537
(800) 342-2086
Open year-round

Sight of (our most memorable meals) & recommended for your now? future

Hemingway's

HEMINGWAY'S

Route 4,
Killington, VT 05751
(802) 422-3886
Dinner, Wednesday-Sunday
from 6:00 p.m.
Open year-round

❧

"ONE OF THE TOP 25
RESTAURANTS IN AMERICA.
THE FOOD IS SUPERB AND
THE SERVICE IS ATTENTIVE
WITHOUT BEING INTRUSIVE,
THE WINE LISTS ARE WELL
SELECTED AND FAIRLY
PRICED, AND THE SETTINGS
ARE ALL ATTRACTIVE AND
WELCOMING."
—FOOD & WINE MAGAZINE
RECOGNIZED AS THE
"ACADEMY AWARDS" OF THE
INDUSTRY,
"THE TOP 25"
WERE ANNOUNCED ON
JUNE 21, 1992 AT THE ASPEN
FOOD & WINE CLASSIC,
IN COLORADO.
HEMINGWAY S IS THE ONLY
NEW ENGLAND
RESTAURANT TO RECEIVE
THIS AWARD.
CONGRATULATIONS
HEMINGWAY'S!

HEMINGWAY'S, INSPIRED by the famed author and trencherman, is considered by many to be the best restaurant north of New York City. To back this up, it is the only four-star and four-diamond eating establishment in northern New England. The setting, food, service, wine list, and atmosphere summon visions of a sumptuous French countryside restaurant. Antiques, locally crafted furniture, fresh flowers, and lovely place settings help make dining in the three distinctively different areas an experience you will long remember. The peach colored main room, with its plush chairs, has a modern formal feeling, while a brick-floored, yellow and white garden room evokes a more casual mood. Downstairs, the brick-walled wine cellar has four tables, with crocheted tablecloths and wonderfully tall candlesticks, making it a favorite place for more intimate dining or small parties.

Chef Francis Clogston and the sous-chef, John Foster, create masterpieces that include locally raised pheasant, venison, lamb, and trout, along with fresh North Atlantic fish and other delectable entreés that bring back memories of Hemingway himself. The owners, Linda and Ted Fondulas, bought the 130 year-old Asa Briggs House, a former stagecoach stop, a decade ago and have transformed it into this memorable restaurant. Linda and Ted believe in the dining experience, and although stopping in before the theater is a treat, Hemingway's is truly a place to enjoy a leisurely evening you will not forget.

Another striking feature of this restaurant is the outstanding art collection. Take some time to graze and enjoy the paintings, ceramics, and sculptures placed tastefully throughout Hemingway's.

Mountain Top Inn and Resort

[handwritten annotations: Pretty place + ride — Nice views golf. Alpine Low buzz never fulltime. Hope for a sleigh ride — Some winter.]

NESTLED HIGH ON THE SIDE of a hill on a 1300-acre estate, amidst the picturesque Green Mountains of central Vermont, Mountain Top commands breathtaking views of the lake and surrounding mountains. This secluded, family-owned inn welcomes guests with unmatched friendly hospitality. Four types of accommodation, all with private bath, are available. There are 33 rooms in the main building, and 22 cottage and chalet units, many with a fireplace, are within a short walk.

The meals are wonderful. Down the glass-enclosed semicircular stairs is an attractive bar and lounge on the left and, on the right, a charming candlelit dining room where the excellence of cuisine is renowned. The extensive dinner menu features such fine dishes as medallions of pork loin, sautéed scallops with chutney, vegetarian alfredo, and filet mignon. The wine list is particularly impressive. Breakfast selections range from waffles topped with hot Mountain Top maple syrup to mouth-watering eggs Benedict.

An inviting list of on-premise activities, included in the normal room rates, feature boating, sailing, windsurfing, canoeing, fly-fishing, swimming, horseback riding, wagon and sleigh rides, tennis, golf on the 5-hole executive course, mountain biking, lawn games, and even more.

Between the end of March and early May the inn features four different "Murder with a Twist" weekends; the intrigue begins at 9 p.m. on Fridays and runs for two days. Summer and fall feature four Photographic Workshops planned to help sharpen your eye and skills as you learn from well-known photographers. Alternating with this are five-day workshops in watercolor painting as nationally known artists help attendees with demonstrations, hands-on instruction, and critique.

The Mountain Top Golf School is open from spring into fall and has combinations of midweek and weekend programs available.

MOUNTAIN TOP INN

Mountain Top Road
Chittenden, VT 05737
(802) 483-2311
(800) 445-2100
Open year-round

❧

"...70 MILES OF THE BEST CROSS COUNTRY TRAILS NEW ENGLAND HAS TO OFFER...A REMARKABLE RESORT WHERE GUESTS TRULY FEEL THEY COME FIRST."

—SKIING MAGAZINE

Powderhounds

POWDERHOUNDS

*Killington Road
Killington, VT 05751
(802) 422-4141
Dinner year-round
Hours:
5:00 p.m.–10:00 p.m.*

❖

AS P. C. SCHMIT SAID IN
PRACTICAL TAI COOKING,
"WHILE NOUVELLE CUISINE
IS UNDERSTATED AND
SEDATE, THAI COOKING IS
FLAMBOYANT AND FORTH-
RIGHT. WHERE CALIFORNIA
CUISINE MAKES MUCH OF
SIMPLICITY, THAI FLAVORS
ARE UNCONCERNEDLY
COMPLEX. WHERE JAPANESE
COOKING IS PRISTINE,
SUBLIME, AND TRANSPAR-
ENT, THAI FOOD ROARS
WITH ENERGY."

POWDERHOUNDS IS ONE of those wonderful surprises you come upon every once and a while. At first glance it looks like all the rest of the "fern bar–yuppie" joints along both sides of the Killington Road, but just walk inside and see the difference. The bar is outstanding, the dining room is comfortable and inviting, and the paintings on the walls, from a nearby gallery, are first rate.

The real surprise, and the reason you will come back often, is the menu in the dining room. Chef David Levine, who came from Tavern On The Green in New York City, is a purist with an international bent who specializes in the food of Thailand. His meals are first class and unforgettable.

Powderhounds is also well-known and celebrated for its pizzas. It does not advertise the pizzas, but came up with a winner, and can't keep the seriously hungry people away.

David Levine's feelings about this book are that the two things synonymous with having a good time and fun in life are travel and food. He wants readers to take this fun seriously and hopes that he can impart to you, through his recipes, the experience of his travels and the fun he has had.

Do not miss eating here while in the Killington area. The two owners, David Bienstock and Ken Jarecki, are on hand at all times and will help ensure that your evening is memorable.

Red Clover Inn

THE RED CLOVER INN, named for the Vermont state flower, was built as the summer estate of General John Woodward of Washington. D.C. over 150 years ago. It's located in a secluded, panoramic mountain setting a quarter of a mile off Route 4 in Mendon, Vermont, just a few miles down the road from Pico Peak. The inn has 15 attractive bedrooms, each with private bath and a view. Ten of the bedrooms are in the main house and five are next door in the Plum Tree House, a converted carriage barn. There is a large and comfortable old-fashioned living room complete with a fieldstone fireplace, and next to it is small but very serviceable and attractive pub-style bar.

Three dining rooms create a pleasant setting for enjoying the Continental style menu that changes daily. The homemade soups are a specialty of the house, or you might start with salmon smoked in the kitchen's own smoker, or the fettucine aux crevette. Delicious entrée choices normally include lamb, roast duckling, pork, beef, and several fish selections.

The Red Clover Inn is a popular place for private parties and functions. The innkeepers John and Lillian Faller, recently arrived from Minnesota, go out of their way to keep the ambience inviting.

RED CLOVER INN

Woodward Road
Mendon, VT 05701
(802)775-2290
(800)752-0571
Open year-round for lodging
Tuesday–Saturday
for dinner

Tulip Tree Inn

TULIP TREE INN

*Chittenden Dam Road
Chittenden, VT 05737
(802) 483-6213
Open year-round*

THIS DELIGHTFUL INN was once a rambling country home of William S. Barstow, one of Thomas Edison's collaborators. A man of means, he and his family came here 80 years ago to enjoy life in the mountains, away from the rush of the city. He clearly chose well, for the Tulip Tree Inn is a refreshing step back in time. The inn has eight praiseworthy bedrooms with modern, private baths, five with jacuzzis. You can easily reach the inn from Rutland or the Killington/Pico area, but since it's off the beaten track in a quiet valley of the Green Mountain National Forest, you'd best call one of the innkeepers, Ed and Rosemary McDowell, for directions.

You can walk the country lanes or go down to the tree-lined trout stream, and disappear for the day. If you crave more strenuous activity, you can hike, bike, canoe, swim, play golf or tennis, or ride a horse all day long. And, of course, antique shops, summer theater, and art festivals abound in this part of Vermont. The skier will have some of the best of New England skiing at the nearby mountains just minutes from the inn. Then, at day's end, you can relax in the hot tub and/or enjoy yourself in front of the roaring fire.

Dining is very special here. Rosemary takes great pride and special care with the dining room setting and the meals she prepares each day. They offer a full Vermont-style country breakfast, homemade sweet rolls and breads, and buttermilk pancakes. The evening meals are particularly special. The homemade soups hit the spot, the appetizers are first rate, and the entrees will satisfy the fussiest critics. The inn won the 1991 Wine Spectator Award of Excellence. One of the many reasons people frequently return to the Tulip Tree Inn, besides the unforgettable dining experience, is the fantastic Library Pub. This small and wonderfully designed bar is as pleasant a place to unbend as we have ever seen.

The Vermont Inn

THE VERMONT INN is a small 1840 country inn surrounded by the Green Mountains and spectacular views of them. Judd and Susan Levy purchased it in 1988 and have substantially renovated the public areas while maintaining the charm of the building. The original wood beams are exposed in the living room, where you can listen to classical music or watch television and enjoy the warmth of the fireplace. The lounge offers an intimate setting with a wood stove and beautiful mountain vistas. The 16 individually decorated bed rooms are cozy and have either queen size or double beds, and most of the rooms have a private bath. Other amenities include a sauna, hot tub, tennis court, and swimming pool.

The restaurant has won the first place award for fine dining in the 1990 and the 1991 Killington/Korbel Champagne Dine Around Contest. The extensive menu features New England and Continental cuisine, all especially prepared by the locally renowned chef, Steve Hatch. In the winter you dine at candlelit tables by a roaring fire in the huge fieldstone fireplace, while in the summer you can enjoy air-conditioned dining in front of large picture windows and take in those gorgeous Green Mountain views.

THE VERMONT INN

Route 4
Killington, VT 05751
(802) 775-0708
(800) 541-7795

Open year-round. Dining room closed Monday nights.

Thai Style Coconut Curry

PER SERVING:

1 can coconut milk
Small jar or can of Thai
*   style curry paste*
Potatoes
Onion
Rice
Vegetable of your choice

❀

COCONUT AND CURRY PASTE
ARE TWO INGREDIENTS
FOUND IN ALMOST EVERY
CORNER OF THAILAND. THE
VARIETY OF STYLES FOR
SERVING THE TWO ARE
EQUAL ONLY TO THE
NUMBER OF CHEFS IN THE
LAND OF SMILES. THE
SIMPLE COMBINATION OF
THESE TWO INGREDIENTS
FORMS THE BASIS OF A
GOOD THAI MEAL,
BREAKFAST, LUNCH, OR
DINNER, WHATEVER THE
HOUR.

The recipe is a simple one that depends on product availability and not so much on cooking skills. Go to your local grocer's Chinese or ethnic food section and purchase a can of coconut milk (not the sweetened coconut used for cocktails). You'll need 6 to 8 ounces per serving and a small jar or can of Thai style curry paste, red, green, or yellow. Red for meat, green for meat, poultry, or shellfish, and yellow for chicken, seafood, tofu, or just plain vegetables.

In a saucepot combine 6 to 8 ounces of coconut milk and a teaspoon or so of curry paste per serving. Simmer. Add whatever vegetables you choose. A simple combination of 3 to 4 varieties of ingredients is best. Parboiled and cubed potatoes, and large slices of onion are a good start. Shellfish, sliced or cubed meats, diced poultry, and hot sausages are all great choices. Just pick your favorites and "build" to your own taste.

Serve with lots of steamed Jasmine or Basmati rice on the side. Tofu is also a good vehicle for these "wet" Thai curries. Whatever you choose, this is great as either a one dish meal by itself or in conjunction with a separate dish of broiled fish or grilled meat. Keep it plain and simple.

Powderhounds

Cold Peanut & Sesame Noodles

Cook as many noodles as you need, as described. In a well chilled stainless steel, glass, or ceramic bowl combine the first 3 sauce ingredients by mixing with a spoon or rubber spatula. Season with the chili sauce or lemon to taste.

Add cold precooked noodles and toss until coated. Sometimes a few drops of hot water helps smooth the sauce if it stiffens in the cold bowl.

Turn onto a chilled plate or into a cold bowl. Garnish as you like. Use one or all of the suggestions given. Put fresh lemon wedges on a bed of salad greens or shredded cabbage for eyeappeal. Belgian endive, watercress, and cashews work well also. Good luck!

(This noodle recipe is neither Thai nor Chinese, but a combination of the two. It can be an appetizer or snack, or it can be embellished so that it becomes a lunch or dinner plate.)

Powderhounds

PER SERVING:

Sauce (per serving):
2 tablespoons peanut butter at room temperature
Dash sesame oil
4 to 6 tablespoons warm water
Chili sauce or oil to taste
Fresh lemon wedges

Garnishes:
Chopped scallion
Chopped roast nuts
Crisp bean sprouts
Cold shredded lettuce or Chinese cabbage
Chopped, preserved Chinese vegetables
Thin sliced teriyaki chicken or baby shrimp

Noodles:
Most any pasta from most any country will do; egg noodles, wheat noodles, udon, and soba are all good choices. Have the noodles precooked and well chilled. Coat noodles with a small amount of vegetable oil to keep them from sticking when cold.

Onion & Leek Custard Tart

SERVES 6 TO 8

Pastry Shell:
2 cups flour
¼ cup sugar
1½ teaspoons salt
Zest of one lemon
2 sticks unsalted butter,
  cubed and room
  temperature

Filling:
2 medium onions,
  julienned
1 leek, julienned
1½ cups milk or
  half-and-half
3 eggs, slightly beaten
1 cup shredded Gruyère
  cheese
1 bunch fresh basil,
  chopped
Salt and pepper to taste

Pastry Shell: Preheat oven to 325°F. Mix all ingredients except butter in a food processor. Add butter and mix until soft dough balls form. Knead several times on floured surface and press into 9-inch glass pie plate. Set aside.

Filling: Sauté julienned onions and leek in butter until soft. Let cool and add remaining ingredients. Pour into pastry shell and bake for approximately 45 minutes, until crust is golden and filling sets.

Seven Hearths Inn

Barley Risotto

Sauté onions and garlic in clarified butter and oil (combined) until soft but not brown. Turn up heat, add barley, and toss in hot butter and oil, turning and tossing continuously to distribute oil and butter. Add half of chicken stock, simmer, and stir until chicken stock is absorbed by barley.

Continue to add stock and simmer, allowing barley to absorb as much liquid as it will, until barley becomes tender. Add carrots, celery, cream, cheese, salt, and pepper, and continue to cook until flavors and texture reach desired softness. Add herbs to finish.

New England Culinary Institute

SERVES 4 TO 6

2 ounces vegetable oil
2 ounces clarified butter
1 onion, diced
2 cloves garlic, minced
3 cups barley
6 cups chicken stock or water
2 carrots, cut in large dice
2 celery stalks, cut in large dice
3 cups heavy cream to taste
1 cup grated Parmesan, Asiago, and cheddar cheese
Salt and pepper to taste
½ teaspoon each of fresh parsley and fresh thyme

Grilled Vegetable Lasagna

SERVES 8

1 medium eggplant
2 zucchini
2 yellow squash
2 pounds spinach
2 cups mushrooms, sliced
1 large onion, chopped
    small
2 cups ricotta cheese
5 eggs (omit for heart
    healthy)
2½ cups grated
    Parmesan cheese
1 pound grated
    mozzarella cheese
1 quart marinara sauce
1½ pounds fresh egg
    pasta

Slice the eggplant, zucchini, and yellow squash lengthwise, approximately ¼-inch thick. Brush with olive oil, chopped garlic, and salt and pepper. Grill until tender. Sauté the onions, mushrooms, and spinach together.

Mix the ricotta, eggs, and Parmesan together and season with salt and pepper. Using a pasta roller (#1 setting), roll out the egg pasta dough into long rectangular shapes to fit baking pan. Preblanch until tender and shock in an ice water bath and dry.

Line a buttered 2-inch deep baking pan with a precooked pasta sheet. Begin to layer the vegetables using one kind per layer and topping each with a thin layer of the cheese mix until all of the vegetables and cheese are used.

Top with marinara and mozzarella and bake at 350°F for 30 minutes covered with foil, 15 minutes without. Slice into portions.

New England Culinary Institute

Bacon Mushroom Quiche

Combine flour and butter in the bowl of an electric mixer. Blend with the paddle attached until the mixture is crumbly.

Add egg combined with ice water until the mixture just holds together. Shape the dough into a ball, flatten, and refrigerate at least 15 minutes. Roll the dough out and fit it into a 10-inch pie plate, making high crimped edges. Refrigerate until ready to use.

Cook bacon in a large heavy skillet until nicely browned. Drain well on paper towels.

Sauté mushrooms in 2 tablespoons of bacon fat until tender. Drain well on paper towels.

In a mixing bowl, with a wire whisk, combine eggs, heavy cream, and the pepper until well blended.

To assemble quiche: Preheat oven to 350°F. Place 4 cups shredded cheese in bottom of the pie shell. Place drained bacon and mushrooms on top of cheese, distributing evenly. Place the remaining 4 cups of cheese on top of the bacon-mushroom mixture. Slowly pour egg-cream mixture over the cheese. Bake in a preheated 350° F oven for 1 to 1½ hours, or until a knife, inserted in the middle, comes out clean.

Simon Pearce

SERVES 6 TO 8

Pie Crust (for 10-inch pie plate):
1½ cups unbleached flour
1 stick unsalted butter, ice cold, cut into small pieces
1 egg
Approximately ¼ cup ice water

Filling:
1½ pounds bacon, diced (should yield 2 cups cooked bacon)
2 cups mushrooms, thinly sliced
8 cups shredded cheddar cheese
6 large eggs
3 cups heavy cream
Freshly ground black pepper

❧

WE USE NITRATE-FREE
BACON FROM JUGTOWN
SMOKEHOUSE IN
FLEMINGTON, N.J.

Spinach Linguine with Arugula & Radicchio Aglio-olio

SERVES 4

½ cup olive oil
2 tablespoons chopped garlic
1 teaspoon salt
1 cup chicken stock
1 cup chopped fresh arugula
1 cup chopped fresh radicchio
1 pound spinach linguine, cooked and drained

In a sauté pan, add ½ cup olive oil, 2 teaspoons chopped garlic, and sauté over medium heat until garlic is lightly golden in color. Add 1 teaspoon salt and 1 cup chicken stock and simmer for 3 to 5 minutes. Add 1 pound spinach linguine cooked and drained well. Stir well until thoroughly mixed.

Add 1 cup fresh arugula and 1 cup fresh radicchio. Mix thoroughly and serve. Garnish liberally with fresh Pecorino Romano cheese.

Serve with crusty Italian bread.

Sweet Tomatoes

Fettuccine aux-Crevette

SERVES 2

3 ounces cooked fettuccine
1 pound medium peeled shrimp
¼ pound sliced mushrooms
½ teaspoon minced garlic
½ teaspoon cracked black pepper
¾ ounces sherry
1 teaspoon lemon juice

Julienne shrimp, sauté in butter with garlic, pepper, and mushrooms. Deglaze pan with sherry and lemon juice, reduce, add cream and pasta. Toss lightly, add salt and pepper to taste.

Red Clover Inn

Pasta Miano

Cook pasta until it is al dente (almost done). Drain, toss with a little oil so it won't stick. In a large non-stick sauté pan heat oil to medium heat.

To julienne basil, wash leaves and pat dry. Place one on top of another up to 6. Roll them as if making a tube, then cut at an angle. Toss to separate. Add garlic and shallots and cook 1 minute. Do not let brown. Add tomatoes, pinenuts, and basil and toss in pasta and mix ingredients. Place on warm plates. Season with pepper and salt. Sprinkle equal amounts of cheeses on top.

Serve with light red Brouilly wine.

Kedron Valley Inn

SERVES 4

1 pound freshest egg
  fettucine
4 tablespoons virgin
  olive oil
2 tablespoons shallots
  finely chopped
2 tablespoons garlic finely
  chopped
½ cup roasted pinenuts
12 large fresh basil
  leaves, julienne
4 tomatoes blanched,
  peeled, seeded, and
  chopped
½ cup Reggiano
  Parmesan cheese (or
  good imported cheese)
½ cup herbed chèvre
  cheese
Fresh ground black pepper
Salt

Lasagna al Forno

SERVES 10

Meat Sauce:
1 red onion, sliced
2 cloves garlic, chopped
    fine
5 tablespoons olive oil
1 large carrot, shredded
1 celery rib, shredded
6 sprigs Italian parsley,
    chopped fine

¼ pound ground pork
½ pound ground beef
½ pound ground chicken
    breast
¼ pound ground veal
    (optional)
2 cups Italian tomatoes,
    chopped fine
2 cups chicken broth
    (homemade)
¼ cup fresh or dried
    porcini mushrooms
    (wild mushrooms)

Cream Sauce:
6 tablespoons sweet
    butter
½ cup all-purpose flour
3 cups milk
Salt
Pepper
Nutmeg

Meat sauce: Sauté the red onion and garlic in olive oil until golden yellow, and then add the carrot, celery, and parsley.

Sauté the ground pork, beef, chicken breast, and veal for 5 minutes, then add the tomatoes, chicken broth, and mushrooms.

Cover, and when the meat sauce is cooked 1½ hours, cool for 1 hour before using.

Cream sauce: Melt butter in a saucepan over low flame. When butter has reached the frothing point add flour, mix well. Cook until golden brown. Remove from heat and let rest for 15 minutes.

Heat the milk in another pan until close to boil, but do not boil! Put butter and flour saucepan back to the flame and add all the hot milk, mixing with a whisk until the boiling point. Add salt, pepper, and nutmeg to taste. Stir while the sauce is cooking for 5 minutes.

Pasta: In a mixer or pasta machine mix flour, salt, eggs, water, and oil for 5 to 10 minutes. Put the dough in a plastic bag. Bring to a boil a saucepan full of water. Add 1 tablespoon salt. When the water is boiling, roll the dough into the pasta machine, fold the dough into thirds and press down, sprinkle with flour and repeat the rolling and folding 3 times. Move the wheel or number in the pasta machine to #2 (or next number). Pass dough through once. Do not fold anymore, move the wheel or number of machine to each successive notch each time passing dough once until #6 or last number of machine. This will produce a thinner layer of pasta.

Sprinkle with flour if necessary. Put lasagna dish together. Butter or margarine a rectangular baking dish, Pyrex or stainless steel (13 x 9). Spread 3 tablespoons of meat sauce over the bottom of dish.

Cut pasta dough to fit the dish and to allow about 2 inches to hang out over edges of dish. Boil pasta for 10 seconds. Drain over a cloth. Cover the dish with pasta. Spread the cream sauce over the first layer of pasta (thin). Repeat the cutting and boiling of pasta just to cover the inside of dish. Sprinkle with the cheeses to cover. Repeat the cutting and boiling of pasta just to cover the dish.

Spread the meat sauce ¼-inch thick. Keep alternating the three fillings (meat, cream, cheese), covering each layer of filling with a layer of pasta.

The last layer should be cream sauce and cheese. Take pasta hanging over the edges of baking dish and fold them in over the top layer of pasta. Sprinkle fresh parsley and some tomato sauce over to garnish (optional).

When ready reserve in the refrigerator covered with plastic film for about 2 days or preheat oven to 375°F for 30 minutes and place dish in oven for 25 minutes. Remove and allow to cool 10 minutes before serving with spatula.

Buon Appetito!

La Meridiana

Cheese:
8 ounces mozzarella, grated
1½ cup grated Parmigiana or pecorino

Pasta Fresh:
2 cups durum or all purpose flour, unbleached
2 eggs
⅔ cup cold water
1 teaspoon olive oil
1 pinch of salt

Zucchini & Maine Crab Soufflé

SERVES 6

1½ cups heavy cream
2 stock scallions, chopped
½ teaspoon Kosher salt
¼ teaspoon fresh ground
 white peppercorns
⅛ teaspoon cayenne
 pepper
¼ pound fresh sea
 scallops, dry
½ pound fresh picked
 Maine crabmeat
⅓ cup grated Parmesan
 cheese

Preheat oven to 475°F. Cut 6 medium zucchini ¾-inch thick. Scoop out a bowl shaped hole, and place on an oil sheet pan.

Put in a blender in this order: heavy cream, scallions, salt, peppercorns, cayenne pepper, and scallops.

Turn blender on high until running smooth. Remove to stainless steel bowl and fold in the crabmeat and Parmesan cheese.

Pipe into zucchini cups. Sprinkle with fresh chopped Italian parsley and grated Parmesan. Bake at 475°F for 8 to 10 minutes. Drop on a few drops each of fresh lemon juice and serve hot.

The Shaker Inn

New London Rarebit

Combine the beer, Worcestershire, mustard, cayenne, and paprika in a saucepan and heat it until just before it starts to boil. Mix the cheese and the cornstarch and add it to the saucepan. Stir and cook at low heat until creamy. Spoon the mixture over the toast and serve hot.

New London Rarebit can also be used as a fondue with cubes of toast.

The Millstone

SERVES 6

½ cup ale or beer
1 dash Worcestershire
    sauce
1 tablespoon prepared
    mustard
1 pinch of cayenne
½ teaspoon paprika
½ pound Vermont
    cheddar cheese (2 cups)
2 teaspoons cornstarch
6 slices toast

❦

BRAD WHITE, A NEW LONDON GADABOUT AND BASS FIDDLE
PLAYER, SUGGESTS SALTINES IN PLACE OF TOAST.

❦

Fresh Fettucine in a Creamy Sun-Dried Tomato, Roasted Garlic, & Mushroom Sauce

SERVES 4

3 ounces fresh fettucine,
 cooked (see right)
1 tablespoon olive oil
3 sun-dried tomatoes,
 julienne
1 ounce mushrooms,
 sliced
2 ounces garlic cream
 sauce
Salt and pepper
1 tablespoon Parmesan
 cheese, grated
3 parsley sprigs

Heat oil and sweat tomatoes and mushrooms. Add cream sauce to heat and check consistency. Season to taste and pour over hot pasta. Top with cheese and parsley sprigs.

Fresh fettucine:
1 pound semolina flour
1 pound flour
8 eggs
4 yolks
2 teaspoons salt
4 tablespoons olive oil
Combine all in Hobart with hook. Remove and knead on board; should be very stiff.

Roasted garlic cream sauce:
4 heads garlic
1 tablespoon olive oil
1 quart heavy cream
Cut top off garlic heads and rub with oil. Bake in 325°F oven until soft, and squeeze pulp into cream. Heat cream slowly for 30 minutes. Purée in blender.

Cortina Inn

The Wallace Harrison-designed Hopkins Center for the Arts shows the resemblance to his Lincoln Center in New York City.

ADRIAN N. BOUCHARD

MARGO TAUSSIG PINKERTON

Summer street scene in Hanover

HANOVER INN

The Hanover Inn viewed from the Hop

Winter 1948

ADRIAN N. BOUCHARD

Shells on the banks of the Connecticut River

BILL FINNEY

Aerial view of Hanover and the Connecticut River

H/O PHOTOGRAPHERS

Cocktails on the terrace at Home Hill

HOME HILL COUNTRY INN & FRENCH RESTAURANT

Home Hill Country Inn & French Restaurant

HOME HILL COUNTRY INN & FRENCH RESTAURANT

PETER STETTENHEIM

The wonderful Montshire Museum

SHAKER VILLAGE INN

This granite-block structure was the tallest building between Montreal and Boston in 1841.

Any or all wonderful Our favorite visiting place for picnic) Artist-in-residence or music

Aspet, former home of American sculptor Augustus Saint-Gaudens (1848-1907)

Aspet gardens

The Little Studio viewed from Aspet

Amor Caritas

JEFFREY NINTZEL

JEFFREY NINTZEL

Loafing on the Ottauquechee River

DAVID BROWNELL

A peaceful afternoon in Vermont

JON FOX

HANOVER

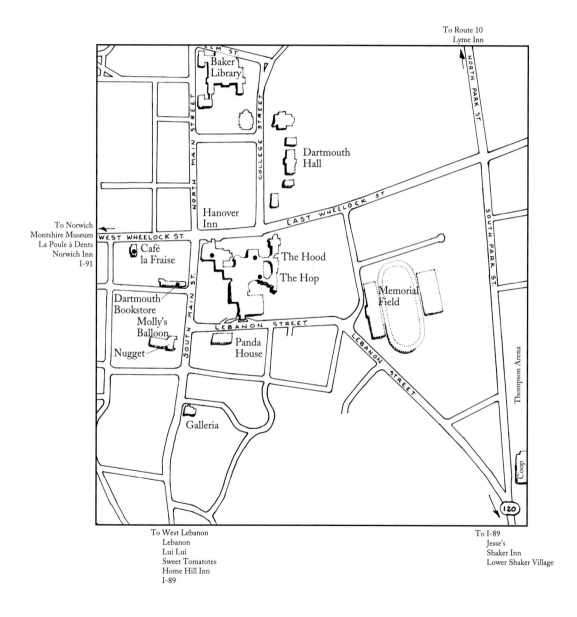

To Route 10
Lyme Inn

NORTH PARK ST.

SOUTH PARK ST.

ELM ST.

Baker
Library

COLLEGE STREET

NORTH MAIN STREET

Dartmouth
Hall

Hanover
Inn

EAST WHEELOCK ST.

To Norwich
Montshire Museum
La Poule à Dents
Norwich Inn
I-91

WEST WHEELOCK ST.

Café
la Fraise

The Hood

The Hop

Memorial
Field

SOUTH MAIN ST.

Dartmouth
Bookstore

Molly's
Balloon

Nugget

LEBANON STREET

Panda
House

LEBANON STREET

Thompson Arena

Galleria

Coop

120

To West Lebanon
Lebanon
Lui Lui
Sweet Tomatotes
Home Hill Inn
I-89

To I-89
Jesse's
Shaker Inn
Lower Shaker Village

Hanover

Nestled in a valley on the banks of the Connecticut River, the beautiful college town of Hanover offers a wide variety of activities to residents and visitors year-round. There is something for everyone in one of the most marvelous New England towns to visit and browse that we have ever seen.

Fall brings the return of students to Dartmouth College, with its famed Hood Museum and Hopkins Art Center, and the beginning of the football and soccer season. And the spectacular colors of autumn foliage make a simple drive through the surrounding country-side a day's entertainment in itself.

"A Dickens of a Christmas" heralds the arrival of winter as this celebration presented by the Hanover Chamber of Commerce fills a weekend (either the first or second in December) with fun and nostalgia from the Victorian era. Horse-drawn sleighs, men in stovepipe hats, women whose skirts brush the snow, and children in long bright mufflers fill the streets and bring back memories of years gone by. It is truly a festive three days of music, dancing, tours, singing, eating, drinking, and shopping.

"The Revels" at The Hopkins Center is a delightful observance of the arrival of the winter solstice. After the students leave for vacation this annual tradition selects a theme and puts on a gala show combining theater, dance, and vaudeville.

Some of the best alpine and cross-country skiing to be had in the Northeast is within a 45-minute radius and, for those less demanding, good skiing is available locally. Winter reaches its peak with the famous Dartmouth Winter Carnival, where intercollegiate hockey, skiing, and basketball, theatre, and the elaborate ice sculpture competition bring people from all corners.

CO-OP FOOD STORE: IF YOU ARE LOOKING FOR THE FRESHEST VEGETABLES, MEATS, FISH, OR ANY STAPLES, DO NOT MISS THE HANOVER CONSUMER CO-OP, A GREAT PLACE FOR HORS D'OEUVRES, PICNIC FARE, OR A WEEK'S WORTH OF GROCERIES. IT OFFERS THE AREA'S BEST SELECTION OF CHEESES, WINES, IMPORTED AND SPECIALTY FOODS, AND ORGANICALLY GROWN PRODUCE, AND PROBABLY ANYTHING ELSE YOU'D WANT IN THE FOOD LINE. THE CO-OP IS LOCATED ON ROUTE 120 JUST SOUTH OF TOWN.

SPRING

"Boiling Today" signs on the many local maple sugaring houses are a clear indication that spring has arrived in Hanover. Visitors are encouraged to stop and watch the sugaring process and then partake in the centuries-old taste treat of fresh boiling maple syrup served on snow with doughnuts and dill pickles as accompaniments.

Warmer weather seems to bring everyone outdoors and the recreational opportunities are endless. The Appalachian Trail passes through Hanover, and the Dartmouth Outing Club makes maps available for the hundreds of miles of walking and hiking trails it maintains.

Do not miss visiting the Dartmouth Bookstore. _Look_ This is a fabulous place that meanders around corners and up and down stairs, and has almost any book you could want. The store is a wonderful resource for anyone who treasures books, and the employees bend over backwards to be helpful. The Hanover Recreation Guide, published by and available at the Dartmouth Bookstore, offers over 150 pages of information on local hiking, biking, swimming, boating, horseback riding, and skiing, plus seasonal events.

The twin Nugget Theater, showing two movies every night, has been a Hanover institution for over 75 years. Both theaters are comfortable and the movies are always current. A quick trip to The Chocolate Shop in Hanover Park across the street from the movies will satisfy any sweet tooth with a terrific selection of jelly beans, chocolate, and other candies.

The possibilities of enjoying Hanover, with its unique vitality, New England charm and year-round beauty, are limited only by your imagination and stamina.

Try?

THE BAGEL BASEMENT AT 6 ALLEN STREET, JUST ACROSS FROM THE SIDE DOOR OF THE DARTMOUTH BOOKSTORE, IS A FABULOUS PLACE TO GET GREEN MOUNTAIN COFFEE, COLD DRINKS, SANDWICHES FEATURING BOAR'S HEAD DELI, AND DELICIOUS BAGELS AND OTHER FRESHLY BAKED GOODIES.

Baker Library

Baker Library is open from 8:00 a.m. to midnight daily.

THE BAKER LIBRARY ACTS as the base of operations for the eight libraries that make up Dartmouth College's library system, and is a wonderful place to visit. When Eleazar Wheelock founded the College in 1769, the library consisted of only a few volumes given to him by supporters of his missionary and educational endeavors. A replica of the library as it existed in 1774 at the home of the first librarian, Bezaleel Woodward, is on display on the west mezzanine of Baker Library and contains over 300 volumes. During the Civil War the library contained 15,000 volumes and the collection grew and moved from place to place until, in 1928, 250,000 books found a permanent home in a new Baker Library, where the volumes now number well over one million.

The Georgian style building, with its 200-foot high bell tower, faces the College green. It houses the College's humanities and social science collections, the College archives, and most of the library's collection of manuscripts and rare books, including a permanent display of Daniel Webster's double elephant folio of John Audubon's Birds of America.

WHATEVER YOU DO, DO NOT MISS THE TOWER READING ROOM ON THE THIRD FLOOR. IT IS WHAT IVY LEAGUE LIBRARIES ARE ALL ABOUT. IT ALSO IS ONE OF THE HIGHLIGHTS ON THE TOUR FOR PROSPECTIVE FRESHMEN.

In 1931, Jose Clemente Orozco became Dartmouth's first artist-in-residence and was commissioned to create a series of murals on a theme of his own choosing. Painted from 1932 to 1934, the frescoes, "An Epic of American Civilization," are on the lower level of the library and depict major aspects of the development of American culture from the migration of ancient tribes to the 20th century. At one time extremely controversial because of Orozco's left-wing politics, the murals are world famous and visitors are always welcome to visit them.

Today eight different libraries house specific College collections in mathematics, music, art, business and engineering, biomedical, and the physical sciences.

This is a great place to browse in; you will be amazed at the classic beauty of the library, how functional it is, and how well used it is.

The Hood Museum of Art

THIS MAGNIFICIENT MUSEUM is recognized by the American Association of Museums as "a national model not only for college and university but also for regional museums." One of the oldest and largest college galleries in the country, the Hood Museum houses over 50,000 works of art and artifacts. Its primary mission is to serve the academic community by giving students and faculty an opportunity to study and enjoy original works of art from both western and non-western cultures.

Museum hours:
Tuesday–Friday:
11:00 a.m. to 5:00 p.m.
Saturday and Sunday:
9:30 a.m. to 5:00 p.m.

A new building designed by Charles W. Moore and Chad Floyd of Centerbrook Architects opened in 1985 and is widely considered to be one of the finest museums completed in recent years. It includes 12,000 square feet of exhibition space, a collection study room, a seminar room, and a 200-seat auditorium.

The Dartmouth collection represents nearly every area of art history and ethnography. It is particularly strong in African and Native American art, early American silver, 19th and 20th century American painting, Old Masters, and 19th and 20th-century prints, and modern art.

The Hood Museum seeks to make a significant contribution to the understanding of the theory and history of the arts and their relation to the broader cultural context through use of the collections and a balanced program of exhibitions, publications, and educational services. Exhibitions have included the graphic work of Rembrandt, Goya, and Whistler, a survey of White Mountain landscapes of the 19th and 20th centuries, surveys of Chinese art and Islamic art, the art of Cameroon, and the art of the Northwest coast and Plains Indians.

A variety of interpretive programs are offered to make the collections of the museum and the themes explored in the exhibitions more accessible to the public.

Great with Kids

Montshire Museum of Science

MONTSHIRE MUSEUM
OF SCIENCE

P.O. Box 770
Norwich, VT 05055
(802) 649-2200

Montshire is open year-round
Hours:
10:00 a.m.–5:00 p.m.
Tuesday until 8:00 p.m.

The Gateway Shop is open
daily, offering carefully
selected books, toys, and gifts
that are science and nature
related.

BE READY TO BE AMAZED, inspired, and delighted by the Montshire Museum, Vermont's newest exciting place to visit. Located in Norwich, on the banks of the Connecticut River just across from Hanover, it is a fascinating museum for all ages from five to eighty-five. Rain or shine, inside or out, it is a grand spot for a family outing, with "hands-on" exhibits encouraging everyone to touch, explore, and learn.

You'll get to see and know more about wildlife and plants from nearby as well as around the world. The aquariums will have you diving into the remarkable realms of snapping turtles, salmon, sea anemones, and more. Many other lively programs and exhibits will show you the wonders of nature, space, and technology. You can spend an hour, for example, gazing at the enormous leafcutter ant complex of plexiglass houses connected by tubes, watching thousands of ants performing their tasks or trying to find the queen ant. The snake lover in your family will go bonkers over Stanley and Victor, two resident boa constrictors who are let out of their living quarters frequently during the day so that groups may get up close and learn about their habits and, if they wish, actually touch them.

Step right up! Get your cabbage stew here, see the raisins dance, make a battery out of potatoes, or launch a rocket. These are some of the many activities that take place at Montshire's Soda Fountain. Every time the start of a new experiment is announced, crowds fill up the dozen stools plus the spaces beyond, all hands eager to make sundials, pocket kites, or "fossils," or play with sound, rockets, or paper airplanes of uncommon design. As a staff member said, "The purpose of the Soda Fountain is not so much to teach facts, but to get people to think about the science around us."

The Physics Playground combines the laws of physics with outdoor fun. Swings, spinning platforms, and other activities captivate all participants, and you'll be surprised at how many simple everyday things are based on the principles of physics.

Montshire's nature preserve encourages visitors to discover the natural world at their own pace. Over 100 acres of trails and woodland along the Connecticut River form a natural backdrop to a wide range of outdoor activities. Fox, grouse, moose, and deer are but a few of the many animals that have been spotted along the Museum's trails. The variety of plantlife is extraordinary and bird watching in the woods and along the riverbank is excellent, too.

Among the many interesting programs at Montshire are "camp-ins," when children stay in the musuem overnight. Since the launching of this program two years ago, over 2,500 kids have taken over the Museum for nights of fun and learning (and even some sleep). Other programs include Earth Day, the Montshire Auction, Summer Sports Exchange, Sky High Summer Day, Summertime Preschool Camp, and Montshire Day Camp. The Lake Sunapee Ecology Study has two five-day sessions in August where visitors travel lake by pontoon boat, sampling the water and studying its plant and animal life, and then travel by van and foot up the tributaries to discover what is happening in the lake's watershed.

The Museum moved to a new building and grounds just over two years ago, and the entire facility is friendly and enchanting. Last year over 100,000 visitors took advantage of this truly uncommon experience.

Lower Shaker Village

LOWER SHAKER
VILLAGE

Route 4A
Enfield, NH 03748
Visitor information:
(603) 632-4346

⚜

DANA ROBES
WOOD CRAFTSMEN:
DISCOVER THE BEAUTY AND
SIMPLICITY OF SHAKER
FURNITURE BEING MADE
TODAY IN THE WORKSHOP
OF DANA ROBES
CRAFTSMEN. LOCATED IN A
SHAKER-INSPIRED BUILDING
AT LOWER SHAKER VILLAGE,
ITS SHOWROOM FEATURES
CHAIRS, TABLES,
SIDEBOARDS, BEDS, DOORS,
AND OTHER PIECES MADE
INDIVIDUALLY ON THE
PREMISES WITH THE
HIGHEST POSSIBLE QUALITY
IN WORKMANSHIP
AND MATERIALS.
OPEN EVERYDAY
(603) 632-5385

WHEN THE SHAKERS SETTLED on this site some 200 years ago they called their community "The Chosen Vale," and today you can still visit and explore 13 of the original, wonderfully graceful buildings. This beautiful spot on the shores of Lake Mascoma, with lots of things to do and see, is definitely worth visiting.

The Enfield Shakers were a religious group who lived together celibately as one large family. They called each other Brother and Sister, and tried to create the most heavenly life possible on earth. Originally called the United Society in Christ's Second Appearance, they became known as "Shakers" because of the violent trembling and shaking of their bodies that sometimes occurred during their worship. The Shakers are famous for the high quality they achieved in all their work: in buildings, furniture, craftsmanship, and cooking. They were pioneers in the imaginative use of herbs, and invented hundreds of delicious recipes. The acres of herb gardens in the Village are testimony to their talents for growing.

The best way to see "Chosen Vale" is to go to the Shaker Museum and Gift Shop, in what was once the Laundry-Dairy Building. After browsing and buying all you want, get a copy of the unguided walking tour and take off at your own pace.

Renowned as the most efficient in the country when it was built in 1854, the Cow Barn is a marvel of ingenuity and common sense. Built in a ravine, the three-story structure was designed to minimize the amount of labor necessary to feed animals and clean stalls. And don't miss the cemetery, herb garden, and the west and east brethren shops.

The great stone dwelling is mind-boggling, built of huge granite blocks that were quarried in Canaan, New Hampshire, and brought across the frozen lake by oxen. We can't tell if The Mary Keane Memorial Chapel is small or huge; it is an amazing structure with vivid stained glass windows, leaded crystal chandeliers, and an ornate altar dominating the sanctuary. The hike up Mount Assurance starting at the Stone Shop is a short walk on a dirt road to the holy Feast Ground and unforgettable views of Lake Mascoma.

The Shaker Inn (Great Stone Dwelling) has fabulous meals and a delightful bar. Very comfortable and handsome guestrooms are available in the main building and two other beautiful houses.

Perhaps a site for a deliberation meal?

Café la Fraise

CAFÉ LA FRAISE

8 West Wheelock Street
Hanover, NH 03755
(603) 643-8588

Dinner Monday–Saturday
Dining Room:
6:00 p.m.–9:00 p.m.
Bistro:
5:30 p.m.–9:00 p.m.
Open year-round

❧

"TRIMMED PORK
TENDERLOIN IS ACTUALLY
ONE OF YOUR LOWER FAT
MEATS. THIS IS A GREAT
HIGH-ENERGY DISH
BECAUSE BOTH THE MEAT
AND THE FIGS ARE VERY
HIGH IN PROTEIN, PERFECT
FOR SOMEONE WHO IS VERY
ACTIVE AND WANTS A
LOWER FAT BUT
HEARTY MEAL."
DEAN COATES, CHEF AT
CAFÉ LA FRAISE.

HANOVER'S CAFÉ LA FRAISE, located on the road to Norwich, is just a block from the Dartmouth Green in an 1820, two-story yellow house that, in fair weather, has lovely flowers growing in the window boxes. There are three intimate and graceful candlelit dining rooms on the first floor, with the smaller one available for private gatherings of up to 15 or so. Upstairs, in a fabulous out-of-the-way bar, is the Bistro, the perfect spot for a less formal and quicker meal before going to the Nugget (Hanover's moviehouse) or a function at the Hopkins Center.

The chef, Dean Coates, is a genius with food and prepares some of the finest meals in the Upper Valley. He was born in England, but grew up in Montreal. He started working in restaurant kitchens at the age of 16. His formal culinary training was done at Le Cordon Bleu in England. Before coming to Café la Fraise as head chef he worked in California under Wolfgang Puck and Bernard Dervieur.

The menu changes often and will usually feature six to eight first courses, the same number of entrées, and always a Chef's special selected and prepared daily. A starter such as timbale of lobster and crab wrapped in smoked salmon with herbed creme fraiche, followed by roast duckling with a cassis and blackberry sauce in company with a superb bottle of wine, and ending with an outrageous dessert, makes for an evening of truly fine dining. The owner, Lynn B. Smith, is ever present and ever pleasant in making sure everything at Café la Fraise is to your liking.

The Hanover Inn

Lunch w/ Claire + Ted
Nice rockers on porch!

AT THE TOP OF MAIN STREET, right at the south end of the Dartmouth Green, next to the Hopkins Art Center, this venerable inn is at the center of everything that goes on in this marvelous Ivy League town. There has been a tavern with guest rooms on the site for over 200 years, but it was not until 1903 that it became The Hanover Inn. The last major renovation took place 25 years ago and now there are 101 comfortable guest rooms and suites, three distinctive restaurants, and attractive public and private rooms available for various functions.

The guest rooms are individually decorated in a Colonial motif, with cable TV, air conditioning, and many special touches to make you feel indulged. Just to the right as you come in the main entrance is an attractive sitting room that is an ideal place to read, chat with your friends, or just watch the comings and goings, both inside the inn and out on the sidewalk and on the green. In good weather the big rocking chairs on the front veranda are another popular way to relax or schmooze.

Between Memorial Day and Labor Day luncheon and dinner are served outside in the Terrace Room, and what a treat this is. Eating delicious meals outdoors on a warm summer day or evening in Hanover is what New England is all about.

Just off the main lobby is the Ivy Grill, a two-tiered, art deco room with large pots of ivy and wonderful paintings of Dartmouth over the booths along one wall that is one of our favorite places to eat and drink. A striking and comfortable bar runs the length of the room and it is always a pleasant spot to relax. The Ivy Grill features American cuisine with an assortment of starters, soups, salads, and main dishes that will please any diner. The atmosphere is intimate and stylish.

The Daniel Webster Room is where Executive Chef Michael Gray puts on his finest and most elegant meals. This impressive dining room features refined and tasteful decor, and is a marvelous place to enjoy a more formal meal that will leave you looking forward to returning to this gracious inn.

THE HANOVER INN

On the Green
Hanover, NH 03755
(603) 643-4300
(800) 443-7024

Ivy Grill:
11:30 a.m.–10:00 p.m.

Daniel Webster Room:
Dinner:
6:00 p.m.–9:00 p.m.
Tuesday–Saturday
Lunch:
11:30 a.m.–1:30 p.m. Daily
Breakfast:
7:00 a.m.–10:30 a.m. Daily

Terrace:
Daily 11:30 a.m.–9:30 p.m.
Sunday brunch & buffet dinner

❧

"THE TOP EVENING SPOT—AND CEREMONIAL CENTER FOR TOWN AND GOWN ALIKE—REMAINS THE VENERABLE HANOVER INN AT DARTMOUTH COLLEGE. HEAD CHEF MICHAEL GRAY, JUSTLY FAMED AS ONE OF THE YOUNG MAESTROS OF NEW AMERICAN CUISINE, OVERSEES THE INN'S TWO RESTAURANTS."
—YANKEE MAGAZINE'S TRAVEL GUIDE TO NEW ENGLAND

Home Hill Country Inn & French Restaurant

HOME HILL COUNTRY
INN & FRENCH
RESTAURANT

River Road
Plainfield, NH, 03781
(603) 675-6165

Open Tuesday through
Saturday from 6:00 p.m.

⚜

"COMBINE ALL OF
HOME HILL'S
INGREDIENTS AND, VOILÀ,
YOU HAVE A NEW ENGLAND
MASTERPIECE WHERE THE
FRENCH ART OF SAVOIR
FAIRE HAS FOUND A MOST
REWARDING EXPRESSION."
—NATIONAL GEOGRAPHIC
TRAVELER NOV/DEC 1990

HOME HILL COUNTRY INN, built about 1800, is a meticulously restored palatial white brick mansion in Plainfield, New Hampshire, on the banks of the Connecticut River. Nestled on 25 secluded acres, the inn offers a unique setting for its three intimate, fireplaced dining rooms. The nine guest rooms are graceful in their simplicity and wonderfully comfortable with large beds covered by impeccable quilts.

Owner Roger Nicolas, who hails from Brittany, believes in innovative French cuisine, using only the freshest and finest quality ingredients. The chalkboard prix fixe menu changes daily but always features appetizers, soup, salad, and choice of four or five main courses. Dinner might start with a napoleon of fresh salmon with champagne sauce, followed by a soup of roasted bell peppers and herbs, and a salad of spinach and endive with apple and curry. Main course selections could include medallions of veal sautéed with wild mushrooms and Madeira, Vermont rabbit braised with wine and tarragon, tournedos of beef with two sauces, or fresh swordfish with aromatic herbs. Chocolate terrine with a raspberry coulis or the house specialty, vacherin glace, make resisting dessert almost impossible.

A cozy library-bar welcomes guests, and an extensive wine list offers the perfect complement to the gourmet fare. There is a tennis court and swimming pool for summer guests and miles of cross-country skiing trails in the winter.

Jesse's

JESSE'S, WHERE THE FOOD and atmosphere are terrific, is the only true steak house in the upper Connecticut River Valley. It's in a large log building, on a hill with lots of parking, located southeast of town on Route 120 near the new Dartmouth-Hitchcock Hospital.

The whole restaurant takes you right back to the "old west." The bar-lounge area, featuring a long L-shaped mahogany bar with brass rail, fireplace, lots of different hanging lamps, a marvelous cigar store Indian glowering in the corner, stuffed couches and chairs, and great paintings, puts you in another world. The place is so loaded with antiques and memorabilia from days gone by it would not be surprising to see a cowboy walk up to the bar and check his guns before diving into the ever-present supply of hors d'oeuvres on the sideboard.

There are three separate and quite different dining areas at Jesse's. Check out the daily specials on the chalkboard in the lobby. The main dining room is in the center of the building and has comfortable booths all around with a terrific salad bar in the middle; this is the more intimate place to dine. The Lodge is a favorite room with its cathedral ceiling, huge log rafters, belt-driven ceiling fans, two canoes hanging from the ceiling, and lots of mounted fish and paintings on the walls. The Green House is a light and airy room filled with hanging plants; it's a very cheery spot.

Dinner always includes the unlimited salad bar (one in each dining room) and fabulous whole wheat sourdough and raisin pumpernickel breads. There is a lot more than just great steaks on the menu, including seafood, chicken, and ribs. For an outstanding steak house with good service, good food, and a different ambience, this is the place to go.

JESSE'S

Route 120
Hanover, NH 03755
(603) 643-4111
Monday–Thursday
5:00 p.m.–10:00 p.m.
Friday & Saturaday:
5:00 p.m.–11:00 p.m.
Sunday:
4:30 p.m.–9:30 p.m.

❧

MARK MILOWSKY, THE OWNER, REALLY KNOWS THE FORMULA FOR HAPPY DINING. BESIDES JESSE'S, HE OWNS MOLLY'S BALLOON IN HANOVER AND LUI LUI AT THE POWERHOUSE MALL IN NEARBY WEST LEBANON. ALL THREE RESTAURANTS HAVE SOME SECRET INGREDIENT THAT MAKES THEM LOTS OF FUN AND WORTH A VISIT AGAIN AND AGAIN.

Lui Lui

LUI LUI

Powerhouse Mall
West Lebanon, NH 03784
(603) 298-7070

Hours:
Monday–Thursday
11:00 a.m.–10:00 p.m.
Friday & Saturday
11:00 a.m.–11:00 p.m.
Sunday Noon–9:00 p.m.
Open year-round

☙

EVERGREEN,
THE NICEST FLOWER AND
GARDEN SHOP WE HAVE
FOUND IN THE AREA, IS
NEXT TO AND CONNECTS
WITH LUI LUI. DON´T MISS
POKING YOUR NOSE IN FOR
A LITTLE BROWSING AND A
HAPPY SURPRISE AT ALL
THE LOVELY THINGS HERE.

LUI LUI, LOCATED AT THE WESTERN end of the Powerhouse Mall in West Lebanon, New Hampshire, is a large upstairs-downstairs restaurant featuring good basic Italian fare. You can't miss the larger-than-life-size chef in white hat and apron out front acting as a lighthouse beckoning hungry diners.

When you walk in the door you are upstairs, and this is the main part of the restaurant. Up a few steps and to your right is the large and attractive lounge with a long bar, banquettes, and tall tables with stools, a great place to relax and enjoy the ambience of Lui Lui. There is a TV in one corner and a few arcade games along a wall to keep you busy before you have your meal.

The main dining room is two stories high, with belt-driven fans and wonderful chandeliers with shades made of Italian tomato cans, and, to add to the pleasure of eating here, you can see the Mascoma River from most of the tables. A huge round, red brick, wood-fired oven for baking pizzas fills one corner of the room. Pizzas are one of the mainstays of the menu and, if you can't find just what you want among the specialties listed, you can create your own "best pizza in the world" by adding any of 20 or so toppings to a regular cheese pizza.

The other half of the menu has such delights as salads (the antipasto is dynamite), soups, and pasta. All of the ravioli, linguini, tortellini, shells, and Italian sausage are prepared daily in the North End of Boston and rushed up to Lui Lui to make sure the meals are always fresh and first class.

The Lyme Inn

TEN MILES NORTH OF HANOVER lies Lyme, a sleepy New England town dominated by a handsome village common surrounded by old, white clapboard homes, a general store, and a large classic steepled church. At the north end of the common sits the Lyme Inn, a four-story, shuttered building that was built in 1809 and originally owned by a descendant of John Alden. This is a genuine, traditional inn—an oasis amid the pressures of contemporary life tucked away among the rolling hills of the Connecticut River Valley. All the fittings and furniture of early America are profusely scattered throughout this homey manor, from old clocks and maple hutches to hand-stitched quilts and even a sleigh from days gone by. There are wide floorboards, original locks and latches, hand-made braided and hooked rugs, and plenty of fireplaces.

Each guest room at the inn has its own special character and is furnished with antiques, ornate bedsteads and bureaus, chaise lounges, ruffled curtains, and fireplaces. This comfortable public house is owned and operated by innkeepers Fred and Judy Siemons, who cater to the needs of the traveler valuing personal attention and a leisurely pace of life.

There are three spacious candlelit dining rooms decorated with 19th century art and artifacts. Control of the kitchen is left to German chef Hans Wickert. Swiss- and German-trained, Hans single-handedly tends the evening fare. The dinner menu's diverse offerings include hasenpfeffer, Wiener schnitzel, Cape scallops, veal, lamb, and prime rib, all individually prepared and served with meticulous attention to detail.

There's also a cozy, intimate tavern with fireplace, original floorboards, and rough pine walls handsomely setting off a grand collection of early hand tools. In the warmth of the summer, the enclosed porch is extensive, cool, and inviting, with bright yellow cushions on its antique white wicker furniture, a perfect place to relax with a refreshing drink before dinner.

THE LYME INN

Lyme, NH 03768
(603) 795-2222

Breakfast daily
Dinner every day except
Tuesdays, Christmas,
& New Years

Panda House

PANDA HOUSE

3 Lebanon Street
Hanover, NH 03755
Tel. (603) 643-1290
Fax (603) 643-1291

Open daily
11:30 a.m.–10:00 p.m.
Friday and Saturday
11:30 a.m.–11:00 p.m.

THIS IS A WONDERFUL SURPRISE right in the heart of Hanover. If you like Chinese food you will love Panda House. Since it's located downstairs in the Hanover Park building, a new three-story brick building just down Lebanon Street from the post office, you will not accidentally "bump into" this restaurant, but don't give up looking.

The several dining areas are extremely attractive with soft lighting, comfortable seating, and snappy white tablecloths. The service is impeccable and, if you're off to the movies or a function at the Hop, fast.

The menu is terrific, the portions more than ample, and the presentation gracious. For lunch we tried #4, #16, and #23; they were outstanding and are highly recommended. The dinner menu is extensive; some of the house specialties that will keep you coming back for more are "twilight lobster," "stir-fried seafood and chicken," "lamb in two styles," and "crispy sesame chicken." With such good food and atmosphere your experience here will be one to remember.

Panda House also has a terrific takeout menu and provides free delivery in Hanover from 5:00 p.m.–9:00 p.m. daily. The takeout phone number is 643-442.

La Poule à Dents

HALFWAY DOWN NORWICH'S Main Street amidst classic white Vermont houses is this beautifully restored, pale yellow with rust trim, 1820 building. Barry and Claire Snyder, chefs and owners, have put together an exceptional country French restaurant where the atmosphere emphasizes personal service and the focus is on outstanding food. You enter the friendly oak-beamed tap room to an impressive handmade, brass inlaid, cherry bar, with walls showing off a collection of works by notable local artists that changes monthly. These first-rate art collections are characteristic of the Snyders' imaginative and sophisticated style, where food too is a form of art.

The menu in the intimate main dining room features four or five first courses, a like number of entrées, and, of course, superb specials. Starting with Peking duck with grilled onions and whole grain mustard sauce, followed by noisette of pork with currants, orange and port wine, a lovely salad, and truffles, is a most pleasant way to spend an evening. For the inquisitive and adventurous, La Poule à Dents offers food and wine tasting where you try a selection of three or four entrées and choose different wines. The knowledgable and diversified wine list is remarkable; countless hours have been spent amassing a collection that offers opulent and affordable wines.

Delicious, less complicated meals are served in the Tap Room for diners with later plans for the evening. When weather permits, outside dining is available. Live jazz is featured in the Tap Room on Friday nights as well as during the sumptuous Sunday brunch. The bar features a collection of over 40 fabulous foreign beers, a large selection of single malt scotches, and armonacs and cognacs that would please a king. And ask Barry or Claire about their private cooking lessons!

LA POULE À DENTS

Main Street
Norwich, VT 05055
(802) 649-2922

Hours:
6:00 p.m.–midnight
except Wednesdays;
Sundays:
11:00 a.m.–2:00 p.m.

The Shaker Inn

THE SHAKER INN

Enfield, NH 03748
(603) 632-7800

Sunday brunch and lunch:
11:30 a.m.–2:00 p.m.
Dinner:
6:00 p.m.–9:00 p.m.
Reservations suggested

IT'S HARD TO BELIEVE that this large six-story, granite-block structure in Enfield, New Hampshire, was once the tallest building on the road between Montreal and Boston. Finished in 1841, it's a classic, grand old place and one of our favorite spots to visit. The glorious granite church next door and the fabulous food, comfortable rooms, and great views at the inn are all reasons to return time and time again, in any season.

The chef, Carl Keller, came here after eight years of training in one of San Francisco's best restaurants and then a two-year stint as sous-chef at 21 Federal, Nantucket's best. In warmer weather his kitchen thrives on the huge herb and vegetable gardens that were established by the Shakers generations ago, and when he can't pick from these he amazes diners with his supply of fresh produce. The food is delicious and the presentation marvelous. Try starting with the smoked lobster and cod cakes, and then choose between a grilled leg of lamb, the fish of the day, or something a little different such as cassoulet of south-west France—a splendid combination of house sausage, smoked ham, chicken confit, and braised rabbit. The desserts are equally good and the wine list is impressive.

Sitting in one of the Shaker dining rooms is a timewarp experience. Original shutters adorn the walls along with built-in cupboards. Lovely furniture, candle-light, and the image of Brothers and Sisters entering through different doors to sit on opposite sides of the room and eat their meals in silence, makes for a bewitching evening.

Painstaking restoration of the upstairs guest rooms is underway, and the new rooms are delightful. Next door the Mary Keane House, a beautiful Victorian step back in time, has four large rooms and a suite with its own fireplace and porch, plus a chapel. Nestled neatly next to the 1854 barn and herb gardens, and commanding a northern view of Lake Mascoma, is Bethany House with seven guest rooms. A private living room and kitchen add family flavor to a home that can be used for individuals or groups.

Sweet Tomatoes

SWEET TOMATOES TRATTORIA is for people who love Italian food. A trattoria in Italy is a gathering place for friends where good food is served quickly and inexpensively. All of the cooking can be seen in the open kitchen in the back of the restaurant. The menu offers fresh, simply prepared, healthy foods either cooked in the custom built, wood-fired stone hearth oven or grilled over hardwood coals. You can taste the difference.

Sweet Tomatoes is located at the northwest corner of the Lebanon town common, on the first floor of a new three-story brick building. You walk into a large, busy, tile-floored room filled with wonderful smells and lots of happy diners. The pleasant art deco murals lining the walls are amusing and, combined with the stylish lights hanging over every table, make for a charming, modern Italian atmosphere.

The recipes and ideas have come from many sources with an accent from the past. The unforgettable flavors of great Italian cooking at home and in the neighborhoods where the owners, Robert and Jim, grew up provide wonderful memories and serve as the basis for the menu at Sweet Tomatoes.

They have captured the warmth of a home kitchen where the bright color of fresh vegetables, smell of simmering sauces, and excitement that goes into the preparation of each dish becomes an essential part of the dining experience. The style of service is simple. When your food is cooked it is served hot and fresh. For either lunch or dinner, Sweet Tomatoes is a winner.

SWEET TOMATOES
TRATTORIA

One Court Street
Lebanon, NH 03766
(603) 448-1711

Lunch:
Monday–Friday
11:30 a.m.–2:00 p.m.
Dinner
Sunday–Thursday
5:00 p.m.–9:00 p.m.
Satuday & Sunday
5:00 p.m.–9:30 p.m.

VERMONT TRAVEL DIVISION

BREADS
PASTRIES
AFTERNOON TEA

❧

Poppy Seed Bread
Dilled Buttermilk Biscuits
Country Bread
Ballymaloe Brown Bread
White Chocolate Macadamia Nut Cookies
Grampa Keller's Lemon Cookies
Scones
Vermont Apple Cobbler
Giant Popovers

Country Bread

Starter I
¼ teaspoon active dry
  yeast
⅔ cup warm water
1 cup unbleached all-
  purpose flour
⅓ cup whole wheat flour

Starter II
¼ teaspoon active dry
  yeast
¼ cup warm water
¾ cup plus 1 tablespoon plus
  1 teaspoon water, room
  temperature
2½ cups unbleached all-
  purpose flour
Mix with a wooden
  spoon 3 to 4 minutes.
Remove to a lightly oiled
  bowl, cover with
  plastic film. Let rise in
  the refrigerator for
  1 to 7 days.

Dough:
1¼ teaspoons active dry
  yeast
⅓ cup warm water
1 cup water, room
  temperature
3¾ cups unbleached all-
  purpose flour
Cornmeal

To start the bread (Starter I) stir yeast into water in small bowl; let stand 5 to 10 minutes in warm room, with no draft or cool temperature. Add both flours, stir with a wooden spoon about 100 strokes. Cover with plastic wrap for 6 hours or overnight.

Dough: In a large bowl stir yeast and ⅓ cup warm water, let stand 10 minutes. Add Starter I and ⅓ cup of Starter II or ½ cup (optional). Add 1 cup water and mix well. Beat in flour 1 cup at a time until dough is thoroughly mixed (5 minutes).

Turn out onto a floured surface (granite, marble) and knead using a dough scraper to begin with until elastic and velvety (10 minutes).

Place the dough in an oiled bowl (not too much oil). Cover with plastic film, and let rise 1 hour (warm place, no draft).

Turn the velvety dough onto a floured surface. Lightly dust the top with flour. Do not punch it down. Shape into a large flat round loaf.

Place on a baking sheet or peel, floured with fine corn meal (muffin corn meal). Turn it again, cover with a towel, let rise 1 to 1¼ hours, or less if room is very warm. Note: Rising too long will flatten the bread; too warm a room will flatten the bread.

Thirty minutes before baking, heat oven to 500°F (if you have a baking stone this is great, but it's OK without it). Score a tic-tac-toe pattern on the top of the loaf with a sharp knife. Bake 15 minutes. Reduce heat to 400°F, bake 25 minutes. Cool bread on a rack. Refrigerate bread up to 1 week in refrigerator or freezer.

This bread is great for cooking, toasting, and so on. Buon Appetito!

La Meridiana

Ballymaloe Brown Bread

Preheat oven to 450°F. Grease 2 loaf tins (approximately 5- to 8-inches) and set aside. Combine flour and salt in a large mixing bowl and set aside. In small bowl, combine the molasses and warm water—crumble the yeast into the molasses-water mixture. Let the yeast proof in a warm place for 5 minutes or until frothy on top.

Combine the proofed yeast and flour to make a wettish dough.

Put the mixture into greased bread tins. Cover the loaves with tea towel and set aside to rise in a warm place. When dough reaches the top of the tins, place in a hot oven for 10 minutes. Reduce heat to 400°F and bake 20 minutes longer or until nicely browned. Remove bread from tins and place top side down on a cookie sheet. Return to oven for an additional 5-7 minutes or until nicely browned on bottom.

Simon Pearce

YIELDS 2 LOAVES

7½ cups coarse ground
  whole wheat flour
3 cups (or more) warm
  water
¼ cup molasses
3 packages dry yeast or
  2 ounce cake yeast
4 teaspoons salt

White Chocolate Macadamia Nut Cookies

YIELDS 25 TO 30 COOKIES

¾ cup softened butter

½ cup packed light brown sugar

8 ounces imported white chocolate

1 to 1½ cups all purpose flour

¾ teaspoon baking powder

½ teaspoon baking soda

¼ teaspoon salt

3 tablespoons sugar

1 large egg

1 teaspoon vanilla extract

½ cup chopped Macadamias

Bring butter to golden brown. Boil for 5 to 8 minutes. After butter has reached color, add brown sugar and let stand in refrigerator for 45 minutes. Grate 3 ounces of chocolate, and coarsely chop remaining chocolate. Stir together flour, baking powder, baking soda, and salt. Reserve.

Remove butter from refrigerator and place in mixer with paddle. Add 3 tablespoons sugar and beat until fluffy. Beat in egg and vanilla. Beat in dry ingredients. Add grated chocolate and ½ chopped chocolate and nuts. Stir until combined.

Roll dough into 1½-inch balls. Dip top in remaining chocolate. Bake at 325°F for 10 to 12 minutes.

New England Culinary Institute

Grampa Keller's Lemon Cookies

Cream the sugar, eggs, shortening, and lemon extract. Sift together the baking soda, flour, and salt, and combine with the sugar mixture. Do not over-mix.

Bake 2-inch diameter cookies at 375°F for 12 to 15 minutes.

For a unique variation of this old family favorite add 2 tablespoons finely diced crystalized ginger and 3 tablespoons chopped sun-dried cranberries.

The Shaker Inn

YIELDS 30 TO 40 COOKIES

1¼ pounds granulated sugar
½ pint fresh eggs
½ pound shortening or butter
2½ teaspoons lemon extract
¼ ounce baking soda
1¼ pounds flour
1½ teaspoons salt

Scones

Preheat oven to 450°F. Combine dry ingredients in mixing bowl. Pour in buttermilk gradually, combining to make a soft dough. Turn dough out onto a floured board, knead lightly for a few minutes. Roll out dough to ½" thickness. Cut into 1½- to 2-inch squares.

Place squares (so they don't touch) on a floured baking sheet. Bake 15 to 20 minutes or until nicely browned.

Simon Pearce

YIELDS 25 SCONES

3½ cups white flour
½ teaspoon sugar
½ teaspoon salt
½ teaspoon baking soda
2½ cups or so buttermilk

Vermont Apple Cobbler

YIELDS IO SERVINGS

6 to 8 Granny Smith
   apples, peeled and
   sliced
½ cup sugar
¾ cup ginger snaps,
   ground finely
1 tablespoon flour
1 teaspoon cinnamon
¼ teaspoon salt
¼ cup chopped pecans
¼ cup chopped walnuts
¼ cup melted butter
¼ cup maple syrup

Place ½ of the apples in a buttered baking pan. Mix together the sugar, ginger snaps, flour, cinnamon, salt, nuts, and butter. Spread ½ of crumb mixture over apples. Add remaining apples and top with rest of crumb mixture. Bake at 350°F for 40 minutes. Pour maple syrup over top of cobbler and bake another 15 minutes.

Bentleys Restaurant

Giant Popovers

YIELDS 24 POPOVERS

4 cups milk
15 eggs
4 cups all-purpose flour
½ cup salad oil
1 tablespoon salt

Heat milk until the edges begin to simmer. In a large mixing bowl scramble the eggs and slowly add the flour until a thick, well-blended paste forms. Add the heated milk, salad oil, and salt and stir until well blended.

In a preheated popover pan, muffin pan (use every other cup for best results), or individual custard cups, fill each cup ¾ full with the batter. Bake at 425°F for 45 minutes, or until the popovers have risen and are well browned. Serve at once or reheat in 300°F oven for 10 minutes.

The Village Inn of Woodstock

Burkehaven Town Hall on Lake Sunapee

M.T. PINKERTON

INN AT SUNAPEE

The Inn at Sunapee

DAVID BROWNELL

Seven Hearths Inn

DAVID BROWNELL

Lake Sunapee from the top of Sunapee Mountain

DAVID BROWNELL

The Inn at Coit Mountain

Lacrosse fans at Colby-Sawyer with Mount Kearsarge behind

SUKI COUGHLIN

Hospital Day Fair in New London

SUKI COUGHLIN

210

The New London Barn Playhouse is famous throughout the Upper Valley for its summer theater.

SUKI COUGHLIN

A wonderful way to explore Lake Sunapee

M.T. PINKERTON

Lake Sunapee at its finest

The Lake Sunapee Country Club golf course

Main Street, New London

NEW LONDON INN

The New London Inn, across the street from the Chamber of Commerce booth

NEW LONDON INN

NEW LONDON

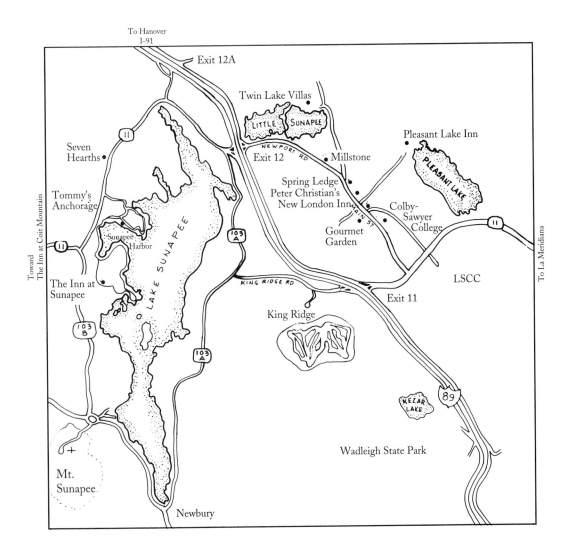

New London - Lake Sunapee

⚜
GOURMET GARDEN,
ACROSS FROM
THE BANDSTAND
ON THE TOWN GREEN,
SPECIALIZES IN THINGS
DISCERNING PICKNICKERS
NEED IN THEIR BASKETS.
THEY MAKE THE BEST
TAKEOUT SANDWICHES IN
TOWN, AND THEIR SELEC-
TION OF CHEESE, FRESH
BREAD, SAUSAGE, COLD
DRINKS AND WINE,
COOKIES, MUFFINS, OR
FRUIT IS UNBEATABLE.
THE OWNERS,
SARAH AND MIKE CAVE,
ALSO SERVE A DELICIOUS
LUNCH IN THEIR NEW CAFÉ
WHERE TASTY DAILY
SPECIALS ENHANCE A
NOTEWORTHY REGULAR
MENU. GOURMET FOOD,
COOKBOOKS, UTENSILS,
GADGETS, AND OTHER
USEFUL THINGS FILL THE
SHELVES, AND IT IS WELL
WORTH A VISIT.
127 MAIN STREET
526-6656

The New London-Lake Sunapee region offers a fabulous mixture of lakes, mountains, woods, and open fields, all combining to present a wonderful variety of things to do and see.

Lake Sunapee, surrounded by beautiful hills and mountains, is an unusually high (1,100 feet) and unusually clear lake. A cruise boat, M/V Mt. Sunapee, offers visitors a most enjoyable and well narrated 1 1/2 hour tour of the lake twice daily from mid-May through the end of leaf peeping and is the best way to see the entire lake. Another boat, M/V Kearsarge, is a re-creation of a 19th century steamer that formerly plied the lake, and provides dinner cruises nightly during the summer months. A full moon ensures a magical evening on the "dinner boat." Both leave from Sunapee Harbor. While you are waiting for your cruise, the Sunapee Harbor Historical Barn will give you the fascinating history of Lake Sunapee's development as a summer resort in the mid-1880s. This former livery stable is filled with photographs and memorabilia of the grand hotels, steamboats, and vacationers flourishing here a century ago.

Mt. Sunapee State Park, on the western side of the lake, is a popular recreation area with an abundance of hiking and bicycle trails, picnic grounds, a large public beach, and an exhilarating chairlift ride to the summit.

For many people the highlight of the summer is the New Hampshire League of Arts and Crafts fair held in the State Park every year during the first week of August. This is the country's oldest crafts fair, lasting for nine days, and well over 500 juried artisans display and sell their beautiful creations. It takes place at the bottom of the ski area in the park and ample parking is available.

Nearby Mt. Kearsarge, with its spectacular 360-degree views to Massachusetts, Vermont, and Maine, is another popular excursion for a drive or hike. The drive through Winslow State Park in nearby Wilmot leads travelers to a beautiful overlook and picnic area at the base of the rather strenuous one-mile trail to the summit.

For the less intrepid, there is a much more gradual half-mile hike to the top from Rollins State Park on the "Warner side" of the mountain where there is also a magnificient overlook and picnic area. If you choose the Warner route be sure to stop on the way up (or down) on the Kearsarge Mountain Road at the Kearsarge Indian Museum—it's a gem of a collection.

The town of New London is home to Colby-Sawyer College, a private, four-year coeducational institution of 600 students founded over 150 years ago. Under the guidance of a very active and caring Board of Trustees along with their dynamic president, Dr. Peggy Stock, this college has grown in size and stature over the past five years to where *U.S. News & World Report* in a 1992 issue said: "Once again Colby-Sawyer was chosen as one of the top two 'up and comers' in the North (a region extending from Washington, D.C. to Maine), the only college in this category to be named among the best for three consecutive years. Our selection was based on a variety of factors including academic reputation, the selectivity of the student body, the quality of the full-time faculty, the college's financial resources and student satisfaction as measured by our ability to graduate the people we admit to our programs."

The Susan Colgate Cleveland Library, winner of several architectural awards, and the Dan and Kathleen Hogan Sports Center, both high on the hill, are two highlights that should not be missed while exploring the campus. Although the college owns 65 acres, the campus is comfortable and accessible, and students can walk to all major buildings without leaving the campus. There are not many college campuses in the country that can beat the beauty of Colby-Sawyer.

The town itself has lots of delightful shopping, dining, and antiquing to satisfy every taste. To make things easier, a map and guide to local attractions is

⚜

KATE SMITH'S SONG "WHEN THE MOON COMES OVER THE MOUNTAIN" WAS WRITTEN BY COLBY ACADEMY STUDENT HARRY WOOD IN THE 1920S. HIS INSPIRATION FOR THIS FAMOUS SONG CAME WHILE SITTING ON THE PORCH OF THE BIG LAMSON COTTAGE ON PLEASANT LAKE WATCHING THE MOON RISE OVER MT. KEARSARGE ON A COOL SUMMER EVENING. HARRY WOOD WENT ON TO WRITE MANY MORE SONGS, BECAME A NOTED VAUDEVILIAN, AND ENDED HIS LIFE IN AN AUTOMOBILE CRASH IN LAS VEGAS. DEBBY PERKINS, WHO LIVES WITH HER FAMILY IN THE LITTLE LAMSON COTTAGE, HAS CONFIRMED THAT THE MOON CONTINUES TO RISE OVER MT. KEARSARGE.

SPRING LEDGE FARM
LIES HALFWAY BETWEEN
THE NEW LONDON INN AND
THE COLONIAL PHARMACY.
PICKED DAILY FROM THEIR
GARDENS: LETTUCES, BEET
GREENS, RADISHES,
SPINACH, TOMATOES,
PEARS, CORN, SUMMER
SQUASH, AND ZUCCHINI,
PLUS QUALITY FRUITS
AND VEGETABLES
FROM THE MARKET.
LOOK FOR A WIDE SELECTON
OF PERENNIALS AND
ANNUALS TO BEAUTIFY
YOUR HOME.

available at the New London Chamber of Commerce information booth on Main Street, opposite the Tracy Library and the New London Trust. Also on Main Street is the famous New London Barn Playhouse, one of the oldest and best summer-stock theaters in New England, featuring musical and dramatic productions from June to September.

There are many pleasant walks and hikes to be had in the area and the information booth should be able to send you in the right direction with pamphlets and maps. One very short but rewarding walk is through Cricenti's Bog, a real bog with a well marked nature trail and many different trees, birds, and vistas. This bog is about a quarter of a mile west of the Post Office on the left side of the Newport Road.

Golf at the casual Twin Lakes Villa 9-hole course on the shores of Little Lake Sunapee is entertaining, while The Country Club of New Hampshire at the base of Mt. Kearsarge and the John H. Cain Golf Club in nearby Newport both have impressive 18-hole championship courses.

Winter in New London means skiing—downhill at King Ridge and Mt. Sunapee and 52 miles of groomed trails at Norsk Cross-Country Ski Center headquarterd at Lake Sunapee Country Club, where delicious meals and drinks are always available.

The Inn at Coit Mountain

THIS POPULAR HOSTELRY is an appealing and inviting bed and breakfast- style inn full of ambience and history. The 1790, white Georgian home was purchased in 1878 by Austin Corbin II as a wedding present for his daughter Mary and her French-born husband, René Cheronette-Champollion. The Corbin family, wealthy American entrepreneurs, well known for developing Coney Island and the Long Island Railroad, were obviously pleased with their daughter's choice of husband. Descended from Jean Francois Champollion, famous Egyptologist and decipherer of the Rosetta stone, René's family had a distinguished history on the contintent.

Mary and René used the house as a summer home and in 1910 their son, Andre, and his new wife moved in. She, desiring a more elegant appearance to her new home, added a 35-foot, two-story library and a large, well-lit studio. Andre, although an American citizen, fought for France in World War I. He died a hero in 1915 and the Croix de Guerre he was awarded still hangs in the library. Their only son, René, lived in the house until 1959 when his death ended the Cheronette-Champollion line.

No matter where you wander, The Inn at Coit Mountain provides the peacefulness of a home away from home. Sitting in front of a fire roaring in the massive granite fireplace in the library, which has beamed ceiling and oak paneling, offers year-round charm, warmth, and quiet pleasure. The five bedrooms are inviting and very comfortable, particularly the two-room suite with its own fireplace and sitting area.

Sumptuous dinners are served to the inn's guests and to groups of six or more that make prior arrangements with the pleasant innkeepers, Judi and Dick Tatem. Judi's cooking talents are well known and highly regarded in the Upper Valley. A hearty New England breakfast of bacon and eggs and coffee cake, or perhaps lemon-blueberry pancakes, is a wonderful way to start the day. The inn is just north of Newport on Route 10 or south from Interstate 89.

THE INN AT COIT
MOUNTAIN

HRC 63 Box 3
Newport, NH 03773
(603) 863-3583
(800) 367-2364
Open year-round

Millstone Restaurant

MILLSTONE
RESTAURANT

*Newport Road
New London, NH 03257*
(603) 526-4201

❧

TOMMY'S ANCHORAGE, LOCATED ON SUNAPEE HARBOR IS THE BEST PLACE ON THE LAKE TO EAT. IT IS AN "ICECREAM—CASUAL-STYLE—FAMILY RESTAURANT" FEATURING SANDWICHES, BURGERS, SALADS, STEAKS, GRILLED SWORDFISH, AND OVER 30 FLAVORS OF EXCELLENT ICE CREAM. FORMERLY THE MAIL DEPOT FOR THE STEAMERS PLYING LAKE SUNAPEE, TOMMY'S ANCHORAGE IS THE COOL PLACE TO GO ON A HOT NIGHT. OPEN DAILY FROM 11:30 A.M.–9:30 P.M.

THE MILLSTONE RESTAURANT in New London, New Hampshire, captures the mood of a cozy country inn with two uncrowded dining rooms, comfortable table arrangements, and its own garden on view through large picture windows.

The owner, Tom Mills, pays particular attention to details. He wants to be sure you will enjoy the little touches that add so much to dining out, such as fresh flowers, candlelight, crisp linen, and first-rate paintings by local artists, such as Nancy Begin and Frances Hoyt, as well as an exquisite American cuisine.

One of the noteworthy and delicious homemade soups is a perfect way to start lunch, followed by New London rarebit or, to choose another unusually good dish, Maine crab cakes. Or you can browse the daily specials on the menu to satisfy your noontime whims.

Dinner at the Millstone is equally enjoyable, and the choices are many. For lighter fare, there are always four or five pasta dishes, including our favorite, "fruite de mare linquine," or maybe one of the pizzettes will be more to your liking. The evening menu is filled with other inviting and surprising selections, and a large appetite is never left unsatisfied here. Venison is always available, and roast duckling, filet mignon, fresh fish, and many other specialties await the eager eater.

The charming bar-lounge area is a favorite place to eat for many of those who come here often. There are half a dozen tables in front of the bar and near the fireplace, a convivial crowd is usually about, and the friendly service and congenial atmosphere make dining here a truly festive occasion.

Tom Mills is also justifiably proud of his wine list; he has taken a good deal of time to create a selection that will please everyone.

New London Inn

BUILT 200 YEARS AGO on the village green, this three-story, white, Federal-style building has been lovingly renovated to provide the kind of country comfort one always hopes to find in a visit to New England. The 30 bright and sparkling bedrooms have private baths, comfortable beds (many with sitting areas), pleasant furnishings, and all the comforts of home. The extra-large, corner bedrooms are a favorite, particularly with those returning for the spectacular fall foliage.

In warmer seasons golfers will find several challenging local courses, and swimming and boating are available in three local lakes. Tennis, hiking, fishing, and biking are some of the other outdoor activities that abound in this beautiful New Hampshire town. The end of an active day will find guests relaxing on the long front porch, in the cheerful living room, or in the large and inviting bar.

The presentation of food at New London Inn is unparalled: each dish is artistically prepared and underlines the gracious ambience of the dining room. Our favorite appetizers are the fettuccine sauteed with duck sausage, spinach, and asiago (a pungent hard yellow Italian cheese, perfect for grating), and the smoked salmon from Maine with a smoked shrimp and horseradish cream. The homemade soups and salads are also perfect complements to the delicious entrées.

The menu changes often and never fails to burst with wonderful surprises. Crisply fried breast of chicken stuffed with goat cheese and basil with a grilled leek and roasted pepper marmalade is fantastic. A lightly grilled Atlantic salmon fillet with a coriander-scented clam sauce and asparagus, or the scallopine of pork sautéed with shiitake mushrooms, garlic, and marsala with wild rice cakes, are two more popular dishes. On your visit to the New London Inn you'll marvel at the selection of wine. The innkeepers, Jeff and Rosemary Follansbee, have put together a collection that is hard to beat. The high quality and the low prices of the wine are remarkable; the wine list even makes great reading! If you have room left to choose from the exemplary dessert selection, feel free to go down in flames.

NEW LONDON INN

P.O.Box 8
Main Street
New London, NH 03257
Tel. (603) 526-2791
Fax (603) 526-2749

❧

IN WINTER
THE NEW LONDON INN,
WITH A CRACKLING FIRE ON
THE HEARTH, IS A PERFECT
CLIMAX TO A FUN DAY OF
SKIING AT NEARBY KING
RIDGE, MT. SUNAPEE, OR
NORSK CROSS-COUNTRY SKI
CENTER.

Peter Christian's Tavern

PETER CHRISTIAN'S
TAVERN

Main Street
New London, NH 03257
(603) 526-4042

Open daily 11:30 a.m.
until closing

✠

ARTISAN'S WORKSHOP:
A GREAT PLACE TO BUY JUST
THE RIGHT GIFT FOR A
SPECIAL PERSON, ARTISAN'S
WORKSHOP IS LOCATED ON
MAIN STREET IN THE
FRONT PART OF THE SAME
BUILDING AS
PETER CHRISTIAN'S.
THIS SHOP, OFFERING A
WIDE VARIETY OF JEWELRY,
ART, WEAVINGS, AND
OTHER WORKS OF LOCAL
ARTISANS, IS WELL WORTH
A VISIT BEFORE OR AFTER
DINING IN THE TAVERN.

LOCATED IN A LARGE WHITE farm house on Main Street in the middle of New London, this country tavern is a great favorite for both area residents and those traveling through who have visited Peter Christian's before and found it well worth a return.

Entering the restaurant you feel you have stepped back in time as the rough hewn post and beam interior with its wide pine floors and booths creates a cozy early-American tavern atmosphere. The bar serves from two sides, with many different beers on tap. The stools are comfortable, and if you are looking for conversation or information on things going on in town, this is the place to find it.

Meals in this pub are fun, as the prices are not high, the ambience is casual, and the food is good. In summer you can eat outdoors on a deck just off the side of the building away from the hustle and bustle of Main Street and in the shade of some wonderful old maple trees.

The menu is typically "tavern" with luncheon specialties featuring delicious soups and salads and hearty sandwiches. Dinner entrées include such things as chicken parmesan, beef stew, and benito burrito. My favorite is the seafood and asparagus puff, a combination of crabmeat, fish, and shrimp mixed with asparagus, celery, and onions in an herb cheese sauce and served in a crisp, golden puff. Wonderful Mexican specialties are served on Tuesdays.

Pleasant Lake Inn

THIS CONGENIAL LODGING PLACE in New London, New Hamphsire, was built as a farmhouse in 1790. It was converted to the Red Gables, a summer resort, in 1878, and became Pleasant Lake Inn a full century later. In recent years the innkeepers, Margaret and Grant Rich, have attractively renovated each of the 11 large and sunny guest rooms with lovely wallpapers, comfortable beds, antiques, and new bathrooms. Most of the rooms have a queensize bed and one has twins. But the kingsize rooms would be my first choice as they have cheerful sitting areas and extraordinary views overlooking the long lawn that runs past the tennis courts across Pleasant Lake and out to the beautiful backdrop of Mt. Kearsarge. Guests enjoy the same amenities that brought folks here a hundred years ago—the lovely lake, wonderful views, bracing walks, and nature largely undisturbed by modern times.

You'll be impressed from the moment you walk in the front door with the tasteful comfort that abounds here. The large, relaxing living room is a perfect place to enjoy the roaring fire, antiques, paintings, and, always, the views of the lake and the mountain. An enclosed patio porch with a handsome slate floor is a marvelous place to bask in the sun during any season of the year.

The classic oak-paneled dining room, also overlooking the lake and mountains, is delightfully furnished with antiques and is a particularly inviting place to enjoy Margaret Rich's memorable country cooking. She prepares the evening meals and is much touted in the New London area for her carefully selected dinner menus. One of our favorites started with an unusually tasty pasta and bean soup followed by boneless chicken breast with cranberry glaze and fresh vegetables right out of the inn's garden. Desserts are also superb.

PLEASANT LAKE INN

P.O.Box 1030
125 Pleasant Street
New London, NH 03257
(603) 526-6271
(800) 626-4907

Pleasant Lake Inn is appropriate for children eight years and older. Smoking is permitted only in common rooms, and there are no accommodations for pets.

Seven Hearths

SEVEN HEARTHS

Old Route 11
Sunapee, NH 03782
(603) 763-5657

Dinner:
Wednesday–Sunday
From 6:00 p.m.
Reservations required

THIS LOVELY COUNTRY INN is located on a hill in five private acres overlooking Lake Sunapee and Mt. Sunapee and is within a few minutes of the State Park beach and ski area, Sunapee Harbor, and New London. Seven Hearths is a spacious 200-year-old country house that has been refurbished throughout with the single thought of making guests as comfortable as possible.

Laraine Pedrero, a successful businesswoman from New York City, decided that breathtaking scenery and starlit nights were to be her new environment and, after searching throughout the area for the perfect location, bought Seven Hearths in the spring of 1992. One of her first priorities was to redo the ten bedrooms. The wide-board pine floors were sanded and sealed, the woodwork repainted, air conditioners installed, and the bathrooms in each bedroom totally modernized. New beds, curtains, and furnishings are found throughout, and in five of the rooms there is a working fireplace.

The dining room has also been redone, and the new air-conditioning will guarantee comfortable summer meals. The new menu continues to feature first-class food. Complimentary hors d'oeuvres are a great way to start dinner, either at the table or over cocktails in the lovely living room with a large fieldstone fireplace and a grand piano. A favorite appetizer is the fresh New England crab cakes with a dilled lobster shallot sauce, and, for an entrée, choose between the Delmonico steak au poivre or the roasted duckling Chinoise. The inviting wine list will add to the meal's pleasure, and the desserts are wicked.

A screened porch out front is a great place to sit and enjoy the surroundings, as is the patio off to the side of the building overlooking the lake. The full-size swimming pool near the beautiful flower gardens is a wonderful spot to cool off and relax. Fresh vegetables also fill gardens nearby, helping guests to remember they are in the country at a place to enjoy gracious living.

The Inn at Sunapee

THIS 1875 CONVERTED farmhouse sits high on a hill commanding a view over a large pasture and woods and running down to Lake Sunapee with majestic Mt. Sunapee as the background. Ted and Susan Harriman became the new owners in 1989 and their gracious and pleasant ways ensure that visitors can come here, throw away their worries, and enjoy the comfort, relaxation, and style of country living.

Accommodations in the main house consist of 12 double rooms, each with a modern bathroom, plus a nice size comfortable reading room/lounge with television. The views from the bedrooms facing the mountain are unparalled, so when you are calling for reservations try to get one. There is a lodge in the large field behind the main house that has three two-bedroom suites perfect for groups or families. You can drive right up to them and there is plenty of space about to enjoy resting on the porch furniture or out on the lawn. A large swimming pool is nearby as well as a tennis court and shuffleboard and volleyball areas. The old milkhouse on the farm has been turned into a cozy, self-contained, pine-paneled cottage that is ideal as a honeymoon suite.

What was once the barn has been delightfully made over into a large combination country living room and lounge. An inviting fieldstone fireplace dominates one end of this captivating room, a hefty bar runs along another wall, and lots of comfortable furniture fills the room so everyone can enjoy the unforgettable view.

The meals here are excellent. Breakfasts are just what the doctor ordered as hearty New England country fare. Dinners are outstanding, too, and often reflect the Harrimans' 29 years in the Far East and Indonesia. The menu suggests, for example, an appetizer of Chinese spring rolls followed by medallions of pork Singapore. Shrimp Santorini, veal with a caper and pinenut sauce, or the chef's ribeye special are other favorites.

Children over eight are welcomed, but they must dine prior to 5:30 to make way for the adult portion of the evening.

THE INN AT SUNAPEE

Burkehaven Hill Road
P.O. Box 336
Sunapee, NH 03782
(603) 763-4444
Open year-round

BRUNCH

Raspberry & Blueberry
  Coffeecake
Ricotta Pancakes
Breast of Chicken
  au Champagne
Homemade Granola
French Toast
Pepper Jelly
Liver Pâté
Breakfast Scones
Salmon Mousse
Creamy Scrambled Eggs
  with Goat Cheese,
  Sundried Tomatoes,
  & Basil
Biscuits
Bloody Miracles

VERMONT TRAVEL DIVISION

Raspberry & Blueberry Coffeecake

Cream sugar and butter in mixer using a paddle. Add the eggs in pairs. Mix 1 minute, add sour cream, then add remaining dry ingredients. Mix for 3 minutes until smooth.

Place ½ of the cake mix in a buttered baking dish. Add raspberries and blueberries. Cover with remaining mixture. Top coffeecake with topping and bake at 325°F for 1 to 1½ hours or until a knife comes out clean.

Topping: Cream butter and sugar. Add remaining ingredients and mix until smooth.

Bentleys Restaurant

SERVES 24

4 cups sugar
1½ cups butter
6 eggs
3 cups sour cream
8 cups flour
3 tablespoons baking
   powder
1½ teaspoons salt
2 cups raspberries
2 cups blueberries

Topping:
2 cups sugar
1⅓ cups flour
2 teaspoons cinnamon
½ teaspoon salt
1 cup butter

Ricotta Pancakes

Separate eggs and whip whites. Set whites aside. Mix all other ingredients thoroughly. Fold in whites. Bake on preheated griddle. You can "stuff" with blueberries or sliced bananas. Use a fork with spatula to help turn over. Serve with real Vermont maple syrup.

The Jackson House

SERVES 2

1 teaspoon baking
   powder
1 pinch salt
3 eggs
½ pound ricotta
⅔ cup milk
½ cup flour
Capful of almond extract

Breast of Chicken au Champagne

SERVES 4

4 chicken breasts (singles),
    skinned and boned
¼ cup flour
½ teaspoon pepper
½ cup butter
½ pound mushrooms,
    sliced
1 cup heavy cream
¼ cup champagne
    (preferably fine French)
4 poached eggs (4 minutes)
Fettucini for 4

Pound chicken breasts between wax paper until slightly flat. Dredge in flour, salt, and pepper mixture. Shake off excess. Heat butter in large skillet and brown chicken on both sides over low heat.

Add the mushrooms, making certain they are in the butter, cover and cook over low heat for 10 minutes. Drain off excess butter (important). Add cream, and simmer covered for 10 minutes.

Transfer chicken to warm plate and hold. Add to skillet the champagne, bring to rapid boil, and cook until sauce is thick and creamy. If too thick, add a little milk.

Place a serving of buttered fettuccini on plate. Top with poached egg. Ladle sauce over fettuccini and egg. Place chicken along side. Serve with steamed-buttered broccoli and rosemary potatoes and ham or sausage. Makes a fine dinner even without the poached egg.

The Jackson House

Homemade Granola

Put the oats in a large roasting pan. Carefully brown the oats under your broiler. Care must be taken to continually stir the oats to prevent them from burning. Keep stirring the oats until golden brown and put in a large mixing bowl. Toast the sliced almonds in the same manner as the oats, and add to toasted oats.

Pour honey over warm oatmeal-almond mixture and stir until well blended. You can use more honey if you like a sweeter granola or less as your taste requires. Add raisins and mix well into mixture.

Eat plain as a snack or with milk for breakfast. This granola can also be substituted in your favorite oatmeal muffin or cookie recipe.

The Village Inn of Woodstock

YIELDS 8 CUPS

1 large container of oatmeal (42 ounces)
1 cup sliced almonds
1 cup honey
1 cup raisins

French Toast

Heat milk mixture until warm enough to blend in the honey (not hot). Add vanilla and honey. Add eggs and whip well. Add to bread on heat pan (turning, so both sides are soaked) and soak overnight. Change to greased pan and bake at 350°F for 30 minutes. Remove and sauté on both sides briefly before serving.

The Vermont Inn

SERVES 6

1 pint half-and-half
1 quart milk
½ cup honey
1½ teaspoons vanilla extract
4 whipped eggs

Liver Pâté

1 quart boiling water
1 stalk celery
2 sprigs parsley
6 peppercorns
1 pound chicken livers
1½ teaspoons salt
3 pinches cayenne
1 cup butter, soft
½ teaspoon nutmeg
2 teaspoons nutmeg
2 teaspoons dry mustard

¼ teaspoon cloves
   (powdered)
5 tablespoons minced
   onion
½ clove garlic, chopped
2 tablespoons cognac

Add celery, parsley, and peppercorns to boiling water. Cook for 5 minutes. Add chicken livers and cook for 10 minutes. Drain, grind livers in food processor, add other ingredients and grind again thoroughly. Pack in crock. Cover with plastic wrap or crock lid. Refrigerate for 24 hours, then freeze. Thaw for 3 or 4 hours when needed. Can be refrozen.

The Jackson House

Pepper Jelly

6 cups (8 peppers) ground
   bell peppers including
   juice (green, red, or
   combination)
1 cup (approximately
   1 pound) ground jalapeño
   peppers
4 cups white vinegar
2 packages pectin
12 cups sugar

Combine all ingredients except sugar. Bring to a boil to dissolve pectin. Add sugar all at once. Return to a full rolling boil; you will need a large pot.

Boil for 5 minutes. Seal in jars while hot. Store as any other jelly. Wear rubber gloves with jalapeño peppers or you will burn hands. You may add a little green food dye for added color. Good as a meat relish or over cream cheese as an hors d'oeuvre.

The Jackson House

Breakfast Scones

Sift together flour, baking powder, and salt. Cut in butter. Beat 2 eggs. Add the beaten eggs and ⅓ cup of your favorite jam (we like peach or apricot). Add about ½ cup currants or yellow raisins. Toss the dough on a floured board, or run through food processor with bread whip attachment, just until dough clings together. Pat into a round shape about ¾-inch thick. Use plenty of flour as the dough will be sticky.

When ready for baking, preheat oven to 400°F. Brush one beaten egg white on dough, and sprinkle liberally with sugar. Cut into as many wedges as you wish (about 8 or 10). Place on baking pan in alternating wedges. (Use a little "Pam" to coat pan.) Bake 12 to 14 minutes. Serve with butter, whipped cream, or Devonshire Cream. Enjoy!

The Jackson House

YIELDS 8 TO 10

2 cups flour
2 teaspoons double-action baking powder
½ teaspoon salt
¼ cup butter (½ stick)
2 eggs
⅓ cup jam
½ cup currants or yellow raisins
1 beaten egg white
Sugar

Salmon Mousse

Place all spices, gelatin, lemon juice, and onion in blender or food processor. Add boiling water. Blend at high speed. Stop and add salmon (drained), mayonnaise, sour cream, and blend until smooth. Pour into greased mold and chill at least 2 hours.

Unmold onto platter and garnish. Enjoy!

The Jackson House

☙

FROM THE KITCHEN OF FLORENCE AND LIONEL BORKAN.

1¼ cups sour cream
1¼ cups mayonnaise
1 small piece of peeled onion
1½ cups boiling water
Garlic salt
Parsley
2 tablespoons gelatin
½ teaspoon paprika
¼ teaspoon white pepper
¼ lemon, squeezed
Chives, chopped
16-ounce can salmon

Creamy Scrambled Eggs with Goat Cheese, Sundried Tomatoes, & Basil

SERVES 4

1 dozen eggs
⅓ cup fresh goat cheese (not aged)
½ cup chopped fresh basil
¼ cup chopped sundried tomatoes
2 teaspoons butter

Melt butter in a large frying pan, preferabley Teflon. Add all ingredients and scramble until done. Season to taste with salt and pepper. Serve immediately with biscuits, crispy fried bacon, and Bloody Miracles (see below) for a timely and simple brunch.

New London Inn

Biscuits

YIELDS 12 BISCUITS

2½ cups all-purpose flour
¼ cup sugar
1½ tablespoons baking powder
¼ teaspoon salt
10 tablespoons (5 ounces) chilled butter
1 cup milk

In a food processor with knife attachment, pulse until dry ingredients are mixed.

Cut butter into small pieces and pulse in processor with dry ingredients until it resembles coarse meal.

Remove ingredients to a bowl and mix in milk. Stir until combined. Lightly grease a 12-hole muffin tin and scoop the dough equally into the muffin tin. Bake in preheated 350°F oven for 18 to 22 minutes until golden brown.

New London Inn

Bloody Miracles

½ cup tequila
½ cup vodka
1 tablespoon chopped garlic
½ teaspoon Tabasco
2 tablespoons horseradish
2 tablespoons Worcestershire sauce
¼ cup lemon juice
¼ cup lime juice
¼ cup clam juice
½ teaspoon celery salt
46 ounces V-8 juice
Scallions

Mix well, pour over ice, garnish with a scallion, enjoy.

New London Inn

COURTESY OF THE LATE PAUL STATEN OF NEW RIVER, ARIZONA

WINDSOR - CORNISH

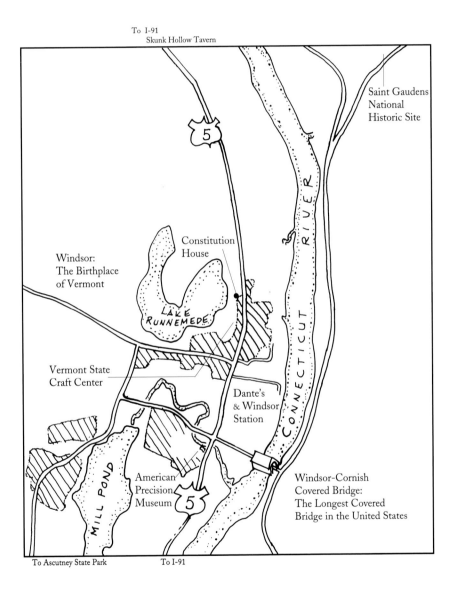

To I-91
Skunk Hollow Tavern

Saint Gaudens
National
Historic Site

5

Constitution
House

Windsor:
The Birthplace
of Vermont

LAKE
RUNNEMEDE

CONNECTICUT RIVER

Vermont State
Craft Center

Dante's
& Windsor
Station

MILL POND

American
Precision
Museum
5

Windsor-Cornish
Covered Bridge:
The Longest Covered
Bridge in the United States

To Ascutney State Park   To I-91

Windsor - Cornish

*T*he most obvious connection between these two historic towns is the longest covered bridge in the United States. The original structure on this site, built as a covered toll bridge in 1796, was later wiped out by high water and ice, as were two successors. The present span was built in 1866, made a "free bridge" in 1953, and was recently renovated. Designated as a "National Historic Engineering Landmark" in 1970, it is owned by the State of New Hampshire, which, by the way, owns the Connecticut River between the two states. Over 200 years ago, Vermont figured that by establishing the border on its side of the river it would not have to pay for river maintenance or bridge construction. This was fine until people became aware of environmental issues affecting the river, such as pollution and new construction, which New Hampshire now controls.

Windsor, "The Birthplace of Vermont," is a fascinating town with beautiful old homes and historic buildings. It has lost much of the commerce that once made it an important industrial center in the Connecticut River Valley, and is now struggling to rebuild. And rebuild it will! There is a lot to see here; the Historical Society has put together two extraordinary walking tours that include about 60 houses built in the late 1700s and early 1800s and the oldest court house and post office in continuous use in the United States. When you visit the latter don't miss the doors on the north side that were specially designed for ladies in bustles.

In 1777 a convention of delegates from "New Connecticut," as the area was then called, met in the local tavern, changed the name to Vermont, and declared it an Independent Republic. It wasn't until 1791 that Vermont was admitted to the Union as the 14th state. This tavern is now known as The Old Constitution House, and is fascinating to visit. You get wonderful feelings and

CORNISH,
NEW HAMPSHIRE,
IS PRIMARILY FAMOUS FOR
THE SAINT-GAUDENS
NATIONAL HISTORIC SITE
(SEE PAGE 242) WHICH
SHOULD NOT BE MISSED
WHILE VISITING
IN THE AREA.

thoughts about what life was like years 200 years ago as you view the tavern's extensive collection of early New England memorabilia.

Windsor is fun as well as a step back in time, and you'll be glad you took that step.

The Old Constitution House, Windsor, Vermont

The American Precision Museum

AMERICAN PRECISION
MUSEUM

196 Main Street
Windsor, VT 05089
(802) 674-5781

Open late May to early
November:
Weekdays,
9:00 a.m.–5:00 p.m.
Weekends & Holidays,
10:00 a.m.–4:00 p.m.

THIS LITTLE-KNOWN National Historic Landmark museum in Windsor, Vermont, houses the most important assemblage of 19th and early 20th-century machine tools and apparatus to be found in America. Within the brick walls of the three-story, 1846 armory is an incredible collection of immense historic significance—the tools that gave birth to mass production and helped make the United States the leading industrial force in the world.

The first thing you see when entering the recently refurbished museum is an entire machine shop in miniature—40 working models of machine tools painstakingly built to 1/16th scale. John Aschauer, of Detroit, spent over 20 years creating this exhibit based on his longtime machine shop experience, and it was all done from memory with no drawings or plans.

The main exhibit is on one of the long main floors of what was originally the Robbins and Lawrence Armory. The floor is of light, polished hardwood, the ceilings and old beams are freshly whitewashed, and large windows create an airy atmosphere to make viewing this incredible collection more comfortable. This room is so packed with machines of every description it resembles a mechanized forest, but in spite of this it is easy to move about and enjoy the wonders of these old beauties. There is an 1853 power rifling machine, for example, that was used in this building until after the Civil War when it was sold to Smith and Wesson, where it remained in service through World War II.

Not far away is a muscular-looking contraption from nearby Springfield, Vermont, called a Fellows gear shaper. Bristling with screws and rods and pulleys and connections and cams, it looks complicated enough to do almost anything mechanical. What it did do, starting in 1903, was introduce a new standard of economy and quality to gear production.

Further on stands a beveled-gear grinder designed by Henry M. Leland, of Detroit, in 1895. He built the machine to make the gears for chainless bicycles, then popular among women who feared catching their skirts in a chain. Leland subsequently got into the automobile business and built both the Cadillac and Lincoln companies before they were bought by General Motors and Ford, respectively.

If you are interested in machine tools you should make your way to this jewel of a museum.

VERMONT TRAVEL DIVISION

Saint-Gaudens
National Historic Site

"A SCULPTOR'S WORK
ENDURES SO LONG THAT IT
IS NEXT TO A CRIME FOR
HIM TO NEGLECT TO DO
EVERYTHING THAT LIES
WITHIN HIS POWER TO
EXECUTE A RESULT THAT
WILL NOT BE A DISGRACE.
THERE IS SOMETHING
EXTRAORDINARILY
IRRITATING, WHEN IT IS
NOT LUDICROUS, IN A BAD
STATUE. IT IS PLASTERED
UP BEFORE THE WORLD TO
STICK FOR CENTURIES,
WHILE MEN AND NATIONS
PASS AWAY. A POOR
PICTURE GOES TO THE
ATTIC, BOOKS ARE
FORGOTTEN, BUT THE
BRONZE REMAINS TO AMUSE
OR SHAME THE POPULACE
AND TO PERPETUATE ONE
OF OUR VARIOUS IDIOCIES.
IT IS AN IMPERTINENCE
AND AN OFFENSE AND THAT
IT DOES NOT CREATE RIOTS
PROVES THE WONDERFUL
PATIENCE OF THE HUMAN
ANIMAL."
—AUGUSTUS SAINT-GAUDENS

HISTORY TELLS US that Augustus Saint-Gaudens, one of America's greatest sculptors, came to New Hampshire reluctantly. He had been a boy of the streets of New York and a man of the studios and salons of Paris. Although, at first, rustic living in a drafty farmhouse held little attraction for him, the old farm he bought in the late 1800s in Cornish, New Hampshire proved to be quiet, cool, and captivating, a perfect summer retreat that later became his permanent home.

Saint-Gaudens completely remodeled the inside of the house, originally built in 1800. Dormers were added, the main stairway moved, rooms combined, doors enlarged, and the upstairs ballroom cut up into bedrooms and baths. The outside of the house and the grounds were where Saint-Gaudens lavished most of his attention. He added the large columned porch to take advantage of prevailing breezes and the dramatic view of Mount Ascutney, and added gables, a sun porch, terraces, and shutters. He finally painted the red brick structure white in 1903.

The sculptor transformed the grounds of his new home from rough farmland and pasture into a delightful series of outdoor rooms and recreation areas. He placed a beautiful formal garden between the house and studio with as many as 50 varieties of flowers. He developed walkways, built a vine covered pergola on the barn-studio and a pool and fountain, planted a vegetable garden, installed garden ornaments, and planted hedges of pine and hemlock.

With these magnificent improvements and Saint-Gaudens' exciting ascendancy as one of the country's finest sculptors, the attractions of Cornish became more widely known. Other artists also found it a delightful spot to spend rural summers working among congenial spirits. Thus The Cornish Colony was born, and a long list of "The Man's" friends went on to important careers of their own. Herbert Adams, Frances Grimes, James Earl Fraser, Elsie Ward, and his brother, Louis Saint-

NATIONAL PARK SERVICE

Gaudens, were only some who worked here and went away enriched by the experience. In 1898 Maxfield Parrish arrived and began to paint those immensely popular scenes with glowing blue skies so unbelievably romantic to many viewers, yet so accurate to one who has seen a Cornish hillside on a July evening when the sky is clear and the sunset has faded.

At age 19 Augustus Saint-Gaudens went to Europe, studied in Paris for 13 years, and then moved on for five years to Rome where he honed his skills and studied classical art and architecture before returning to New York to seek his first major commisson. In 1876 he received such a commission, a monument to the Civil War hero Admiral David Farragut.

After unveiling the Farragut in 1881 in New York's Madison Square, Saint-Gaudens no longer had to struggle for recognition. The monument was hailed as a great achievement, a departure for American sculpture that combined realism and allegory. More work flowed into his studio: "The Ames Monument," "The Puritan," "The Standing Lincoln," all in rapid succession, as well as commissions for over a dozen portrait reliefs. Saint-Gaudens is still considered to be the greatest master of reliefs since the Renaissance.

His greatest achievement is considered by many to be "The Shaw Memorial," completed in 1897 and described as "a symphony in bronze." The Shaw, located in Boston on Beacon Street across from the state capitol building, is a memorial to Colonel Robert Gould Shaw and the 54th Massachusetts Regiment, the first black infantry regiment in the Civil War.

At the turn of the century Saint-Gaudens developed a malignancy that resulted in surgery and led to his decision to move to Cornish permanently. For the next seven years he courageously fought the cancer while continuing to work. His "Sherman Monument" and his memorial to Robert Louis Stevenson were unveiled in 1903 and 1904. Despite his pain and diminishing energy he took on what was to be his last major project. At the request of President Theodore Roosevelt he redesigned the $10 and $20 gold pieces. The magnificent "eagle" and "double eagle" were minted only months after Saint-Gaudens died on August 3, 1907.

"IT SEEMS AS IF WE ARE ALL IN ONE OPEN BOAT ON THE OCEAN, ABANDONED AND DRIFTING, NO ONE KNOWS WHERE, AND WHILE DOING ALL WE CAN TO GET SOMEWHERE, IT IS BETTER TO BE CHEERFUL THAN TO BE MELANCHOLY... LOVE AND COURAGE ARE THE GREAT THINGS..."
—AUGUSTUS SAINT-GAUDENS

The joys of visiting this historic site are boundless. The buildings, gardens, hiking paths, art, and music make a visit to Saint-Gaudens' home one you will long remember.

Sunday concerts are held outside during July and August. Sitting on the lawn and being a part of this experience is a superb way to spend a summer afternoon.

The site is open daily from the last weekend in May through October. The buildings are open from 8:30 a.m. to 4:00 p.m. and the grounds from 8:00 a.m. until dark.

Saint-Gaudens National Historic Site is part of and beautifully maintained by the National Park Service, and is located on Route 12A in Cornish, New Hampshire, nine miles north of Claremont, New Hampshire, and two miles across the Connecticut River from Windsor, Vermont.

NATIONAL PARK SERVICE

Windsor Station & Dante's

WINDSOR STATION
Depot Avenue
Windsor, VT 05089
(802) 674-2052
Hours:
Monday–Thursday
5:30 p.m.–9:00 p.m.
Friday–Sunday
5:30 p.m.–10:00 p.m.
Open year-round

DANTE'S RIB ROOM
Depot Avenue
Windsor, VT 05089
(802) 674-2675
Hours:
Tuesday–Friday
11:30 a.m.–2:00 p.m.
Open year-round

"GO BACK IN TIME" barely describes the old-time atmosphere at this marvelously funky and stylish eating complex in Windsor, Vermont. There are banquet facilities with three function rooms for 20 to 200 people, full service off-premises catering, and a combination deli and bakery that has the finest in meats, cheeses, fresh salads, and wonderful baked goods. But as good as these are, they don't tell the story of stepping back three or four generations in the complex's two restaurants, Dante's and Windsor Station.

The original Windsor Station was built in 1900 and was a thriving train depot until the decline of the machine tool industry in the Connecticut River Valley triggered the slump of the railroads. After being vacant for many years, it was renovated in 1977 to become this unique and captivating restaurant.

Dante's Rib Room is diagonally across the street from Windsor Station, underneath the banquet rooms, and is a classic place to eat. Elegant Victorian decor is marked by lace curtains, incomparable wallpaper, flowers, and great food. The luncheon menu features soup, salads, pasta, a wonderful selection of sandwiches, and, of course, daily specials. I had the open hot roast beef sandwich with mashed potatoes and gravy, with peas and pearl onions. It really is worth going out of your way to have lunch or dinner here; it is a blast!

Windsor Station has a more extensive menu than Dante's with all sorts of veal, beef, seafood, fowl, and daily specials. The pasta Ricardo, an old family recipe of the owners, Rudy and Pat Aldighieri, features fresh broccoli, shrimp, and linguine tossed in a delicate garlic sauce. The steaks are fabulous. You can relax in this beautifully restored railroad station with its natural woods, plush velvets, brass trimmings, and venerable background music, enjoying the Victorian atmosphere with one of the many interesting selections from the wine list, and feel that you have stepped into another era.

DESSERTS

Raspberry Pâté
Three-Ginger Gingerbread
Chantilly Cream
Lemon Curd
Lyme Soufflé
Pecan Pie
Crème Jamaica
Indian Pudding
Pears Poached
    in Sauterne
Frozen Blackberry Soufflés
Pear Dumpling
Bourbon Pecan Cheesecake
Dark Rum
    Mocha Cheesecake
Individual Peach
    Amaretto Tarts
Apple Pie
Chocolate Mousse
Chocolate Frangelico Pie
Brandy Alexander Pie
Chocolate Crumb Crust
Mississippi Mud Cake
Frozen White Chocolate
    & Bailey's Mousse
Warm Caramel Sauce

Pumpkin Cheesecake
Maple Mousse
Chocolate Terrine
Chocolate Macadamia
    Truffle Torte
Vacherin Glace
Apple Pie
Walnut Meringue
Dacquoise au Chocolat
    Meringue Nut Cake
Chocolate Butter Cream
Maple Apple
    Walnut Crisp
White Chocolate
    Cashew Cheesecake
Poached Pears
    in Orange Sauce
Strawberry Soup
Benne Wafers
Maple Chocolate
    and Walnut Pie
Frozen Raspberry Mousse
Irish Cordial Pie
Mudslide Pie
Fruit Tarts
    with Apple Cider Sauce

Strafford, Vermont, the home of Stone Soup

VERMONT TRAVEL DIVISION

Raspberry Pâté

Crush cookies in food processor or with rolling pin to make 4 cups of crumbs. Combine ¾ cup crumbs with raspberries, cinnamon, and 1 tablespoon sugar; set aside.

Combine remaining 3½ cups crumbs with enough cream to hold them together. Reserve 1 cup crumb mixture for top crust.

Sprinkle 1 tablespoon sugar onto bottom of a 8½- x 4½-inch loaf pan. Press crumb mixture evenly over bottom and sides of pan. Gently spoon raspberry mixture into pan. Top with reserved crumb mixture.

Cover with waxed paper. Using similar-size loaf pan, press pâté gently to compact. Cover; refrigerate at least 3 hours or overnight.

Loosen sides of pâté with thin knife. Invert pâté from loaf pan onto serving plate. Slice with sharp knife; drizzle with 2 to 3 tablespoons raspberry sauce. Serve with remaining sauce.

Raspberry Sauce: In 2-quart saucepan over medium heat, cook raspberries and water just until raspberries pop, about 5 minutes. Press mixture through sieve to remove seeds. Add sugar to desired sweetness. Refrigerate until well chilled.

Stone Soup

SERVES 8 TO 10

15 ounces shortbread cookies (1½ ten-ounce packages)
3 cups fresh raspberries
⅛ teaspoon cinnamon
2 tablespoons sugar, divided
⅓ to ½ cup heavy or whipping cream
Raspberry sauce

Raspberry Sauce:
(makes about 2 cups)
3 cups raspberries
2 tablespoons water
Sugar

Three-Ginger Gingerbread

SERVES 8 TO 10

3 eggs
1 tablespoon fresh ginger,
  chopped
1 cup dark molasses
½ cup crystallized ginger,
  chopped
1 cup sugar
1 cup vegetable oil
2½ cups all-purpose flour
2 teaspoons baking soda
¾ teaspoon salt
2 teaspoons ground cloves
1 tablespoon ground
  cinnamon
1 tablespoon ground
  ginger
½ cup boiling water

Preheat oven to 375°F. Butter the bottom of a 9-inch springform pan. Line the bottom of the pan with parchment paper. Butter and flour the bottom and sides of pan and put aside until ready to use.

Mix the first 6 ingredients with beaters until smooth, about 30 seconds.

In another bowl, stir the next 6 ingredients with a fork until well mixed, then beat into the wet ingredients ¼ at a time, and continue to beat until smooth.

Add ½ cup boiling water into mixture, scrape bowl, and mix until smooth, about 30 seconds.

Pour the batter into the prepared pan; drop the pan a couple of times to even the batter. Bake in the preheated oven for 1 hour to 1 hour 10 minutes, until top springs back. Let the gingerbread cool for 10 minutes before removing from pan. This is best served at once, warm, but will keep nicely, wrapped tightly with plastic in the refrigerator, and then warmed in the microwave.

New London Inn

Chantilly Cream

Whip all ingredients until stiff peaks form. Refrigerate until ready for use.

1½ cups heavy cream
¼ cup sugar
1 teaspoon vanilla
* extract*

Presentation:
Cut gingerbread (see opposite page) into eight pieces. Spoon two tablespoons of curd onto the center of each plate. Place warm gingerbread on top. Place a dollop of whipped cream on top of gingerbread. Garnish with a strawberry fan and fresh mint if desired.

New London Inn

Lemon Curd

Peel zest from lemons with a vegetable peeler, being careful not to include white membrane; chop finely. Juice the lemons. You should have about ¼ cup; if not, juice another lemon until you have ¼ cup.

2 lemons
6 tablespoons butter
1 cup sugar
3 eggs

Put all ingredients except eggs into a double boiler over simmering water. Stir occasionally until the butter and sugar melt. In another bowl, lightly mix the eggs. Temper the eggs with a little of the hot mixture, then pour the eggs into the double boiler, stirring constantly.

Continue to stir until the curd is thick, then remove from heat. Refrigerate until ready to use.

New London Inn

Pears Poached in Sauterne

SERVES 8 TO 16

8 large pears (peeled, cored, and quartered)
3 tablespoons fresh lemon juice
1 bottle Sauterne
4 tablespoons sugar
2 teaspoons pear brandy (optional)
4 whole cloves
Freshly grated lime zest

In a medium bowl, toss pears with lemon juice. In a large, shallow, non-reactive pan, combine the Sauterne, sugar, and cloves. Bring to boil. Add the pears. Cook until pears are tender, 8 to 10 minutes. Remove pears and set aside. Discard cloves.

Boil poaching liquid over moderate heat until reduced to ¾ cup, approximately 8 to 10 minutes. Let cool, stir in brandy (if using). Combine pears and syrup. Cover and refrigerate. Serve on plate with syrup and garnish of lime zest.

The Woodstock Inn & Resort

Frozen Blackberry Soufflés

Process blackberries and water in food processor, then pass through sieve to remove seeds. Combine blackberry juice with ½ cup of sugar and cook over medium heat in non-aluminum pan until reduced to ¾ cup liquid. Let cool. Combine egg yolks with 1 tablespoon water and whip hard over heat until thick and fluffy. Add blackberry liquid to yolks and set aside.

Whip cream with ¼ cup of sugar to soft peaks. Whip egg whites to soft peaks. Stir whipped cream into blackberry mixture, then fold in the rest of the whipped cream and egg whites. Pour into ramekins fitted with collars and freeze for 6 hours.

Quechee Inn at Marshland Farm

SERVES 4

4 cups fresh blackberries
½ cup water
¾ cup sugar
1½ cups heavy cream
3 eggs

Pear Dumpling

YIELDS 8 DUMPLINGS

8 pears, slightly ripened

Sugar Filling:
1½ cups light brown
    sugar
½ teaspoon cinnamon
4 tablespoons melted
    butter
½ cup currants
¼ cup chopped
    crystalized ginger

Pastry:
1½ cups shortening
1 tablespoon sugar
1 teaspoon salt
1 tablespoon baking
    powder
1¾ cups milk
2 tablespoons water

Glaze:
2 cups sugar
1 teaspoon cinnamon
2 cups hot water
½ cup melted butter

Sugar filling: Combine all ingredients in a bowl until thoroughly mixed and smooth.

Peel, core, stuff pears with sugar filling.

Pastry: Sift sugar, flour, salt, and baking powder together. Cut into shortening until you have a grainy texture. Add milk, stirring with fork. Use cold water if needed to roll out dough.

Roll pastry to approximately ¼-inch thickness. Cut in 5-inch squares. Place standing pear in center of square. Pull corners to top and crimp together. Seal the sides well.

Place prepared dumplings in freezer for 30 minutes before baking in a 350°F oven, unglazed, for 15 minutes. Pour glaze over and glaze every 15 minutes thereafter. Bake a total of 1¼ hours or until a knife inserts easily into a pear.

Stone Soup

Bourbon Pecan Cheesecake

Have cream cheese at room temperature. Beat cheese adding eggs one at a time. Add yolk and beat until smooth. Slowly add sugar, lemon, and vanilla. Scrape bottom of bowl and beat until light. Beat in flour. Preheat oven to 325°F.

Combine graham cracker crumbs, butter, and sugar well with a fork. Press mixture evenly into a 10-inch springform cake pan.

For topping, place sugar in a small bowl. Add butter and cut in until mixture resembles coarse meal. Stir pecans into mixture.

Pour batter into cake pan. Bake about 1½ hours or until center no longer moves when pan is shaken. Sprinkle topping over the top and bake 15 minutes. Refrigerate overnight.

The Prince & The Pauper

SERVES 12

Requires a 10-inch springform cake pan.

Cheesecake:
2½ pounds cream cheese
¾ cup sugar
2 tablespoons all-purpose flour
1 tablespoon fresh lemon juice
1 teaspoon vanilla
4 eggs
1 yolk

Crust:
2 cups graham cracker crumbs
3 tablespoons melted butter
3 tablespoons sugar

Topping:
¾ cup brown sugar
¾ stick chilled butter
1½ cups chopped pecans

AN ALL-TIME FAVORITE AT THE PRINCE & THE PAUPER.

Dark Rum Mocha Cheesecake

Crust:
2 cups chocolate wafers or cookies
1 teaspoon cinnamon
1 teaspoon finely ground instant coffee powder
1 orange rind, finely minced
8 teaspoons melted butter

Filling:
1 pound cream cheese, room temperature
2 eggs
½ cup sugar
½ teaspoon vanilla
2 tablespoons dark rum
1 tablespoon instant coffee powder
3 tablespoons butter, melted
1½ cups sour cream
8 ounces semisweet chocolate, melted

Whipped Cream:
½ to 1 pint heavy cream
Dark rum to taste
Sugar to taste

Crust: Preheat oven to 350°F. Blend wafers in a food processor until fine. Add cinnamon, coffee powder, and orange rind; blend. Add butter; blend. In a buttered 10-inch springform pan, press dough onto bottom of pan and ½ inch up sides. Cool in refrigerator for at least 6 hours, preferably overnight.

Filling: In a food processor, blend cream cheese until soft. Add eggs, sugar, vanilla, rum, and coffee powder. With machine on low, add butter, sour cream, and chocolate, and mix until well blended. Pour into prepared crust and gently tap pan to smooth. Place pan on cookie sheet to catch escaping butter and bake for 45 minutes. Let cool, cover, and place in refrigerator overnight. Serve with whipped cream.

Whipped Cream: Beat heavy cream until fluffy. Add rum and sugar to taste.

Seven Hearths Inn

Individual Peach Amaretto Tarts

Preheat oven to 375°F. Cream butter and sugar. Add egg yolks and amaretto. Add flour and almonds, mixing only until flour is incorporated. Refrigerate. Roll out to ⅛-inch thickness. Line greased tart pans and bake for 15 minutes or until light brown. Remove from oven.

Combine sugar, corn starch, and flour. Add eggs and mix well. Heat the milk and amaretto until it is just about to boil. Pour over egg mixture and blend well. Return to pan and cook over low heat, stirring constantly until thick. Refrigerate.

Melt 2 ounces semi-sweet chocolate with 1 ounce heavy cream. Cool slightly then brush on inside of cooked tart shell. Cool. Cover bottom of tart shell with pastry cream. Slice fresh peaches and arrange on top. Garnish with strawberry and whipped cream.

The Inn at Norwich

Pastry:
2 tablespoons crushed
   almonds
½ cup sugar
4 egg yolks
½ teaspoon amaretto
4 ounces butter
1 cup flour

Pastry Cream Filling:
3 tablespoons sugar
2 teaspoons corn starch
1 tablespoon flour
2 eggs
2 cups milk
1 tablespoon amaretto

Apple Pie

SERVES 8

Crust:
1½ cups flour
4 ounces cold butter
3 tablespoons Domino
    sugar
1 egg
1 tablespoon vanilla
1 tablespoon cold water

Filling:
8 Granny Smith apples,
    peeled, cored,
    and sliced
⅔ cup brown sugar
Zest and juice of one
    lemon
1 tablespoon cinnamon

1 teaspoon nutmeg
¼ cup flour
2 ounces melted butter
8 ounces fresh
    cranberries

Crumb Topping:
6 ounces butter
⅔ cup brown Domino
    sugar
1½ cups flour
½ tablespoon cinnamon
½ teaspoon nutmeg

Crust Method: Mix flour with butter until crumbly, then add sugar, egg, vanilla, and water. Mix until dough forms a ball. Chill in refrigerator for at least an hour before rolling out.

Filling method: Peel, core and slice apples into a mixing bowl, add the rest of the ingredients, toss lightly and place directly into prepared pie crust.

Crumb Topping method: Mix all ingredients together only until crumbly. Spread over top of pie. Bake at 400°F for 40 to 50 minutes.

The Inn at Norwich

Chocolate Mousse

Chop the chocolate, and in a double boiler melt chocolate and espresso coffee. Stir all together. Beat the egg yolks with the sugar for 5 minutes. Fold in the chocolate. Beat whites with pinch of salt, and fold into the chocolate and sugar mixture. Whip the cream with a pinch of sugar and ½ teaspoon vanilla.

Fold the cream into the mixture gently. Put the mousse in one bowl or 6 small dishes. Decorate with whipped cream (optional) and grated chocolate.

La Meridiana

SERVES 6

10 grams sugar
200 grams semisweet
  chocolate
3 eggs, separated
5 ounces espresso coffee
16 ounces whipping
  cream
Pinch of salt
Pinch of sugar
½ teaspoon vanilla

FROM MARIA ROSA

Chocolate Frangelico Pie

Mix together graham cracker crumbs and melted butter. Line 8- to 9-inch springform pan bottom with mixture.

In double boiler, melt chocolate chips with water. Let melted chips cool to room temperature.

In a mixer, whip heavy cream until "fluffy." Fold in chocolate mixture and liqueur and whip until firm.

Place mixture in springform pan. Chill until firm. Garnish with sliced almonds.

Mountain Top Inn and Resort

SERVES 8

1 cup graham cracker
  crumbs
2 ounces melted butter
2 cups chocolate chips
½ cup water
3 cups heavy whipping
  cream
2 shots Frangelico
  liqueur
Sliced almonds

Brandy Alexander Pie

SERVES ABOUT 8

1 envelope unflavored
    gelatin
½ cup cold water
⅔ cup sugar
⅛ teaspoon salt
2 eggs, separated
¼ cup cognac
¼ cup crème de cacao
2 cups heavy cream,
    whipped
One 9-inch chocolate
    crumb crust (see
    below)

Sprinkle the gelatin over cold water in saucepan. Add ⅓ cup of the sugar, salt, and the egg yolks. Stir to blend. Heat over low heat while stirring until the gelatin dissolves and mixture thickens.

Remove from the heat and stir in the cognac and crème de cacao. Chill until the mixture starts to mound slightly.

Beat the egg whites until stiff. Gradually beat in the remaining sugar and fold into the thickened gelatin mixture. Fold in one cup of the whipped cream. Turn into the crust. Chill. Top with the remaining cup of whipped cream.

The Lyme Inn

Chocolate Crumb Crust

1½ cups chocolate wafer
    crumbs, crushed
    very fine
6 tablespoons
    melted butter

Mix well and pat firmly into a 9-inch pan, covering bottom and sides. Either chill thoroughly before filling or bake in a 300°F oven for 15 minutes.

The Lyme Inn

Mississippi Mud Cake
Front Street (Fudge Cake)

Into a bowl sift together flour, baking soda, and a pinch of salt. In the top of a double boiler set over simmering water, heat 1¾ cups coffee and ¼ cup bourbon for 5 minutes. Add unsweetened chocolate and butter, all cut into pieces, and heat the mixture, stirring until the chocolate and butter are melted and the mixture is smooth. Remove the pan from the heat and stir in the sugar. Let the mixture cool for 3 minutes and transfer it to the bowl of an electric mixer. Add the flour mixture to the chocolate mixture, ½ cup at a time, beating at medium speed and continue to beat mixture for 1 minute. Add 2 eggs, lightly beaten, and 1 teaspoon vanilla and beat the batter until it is smooth.

Butter a 9-inch tube pan, 3½ -inches deep, and dust it with cocoa. Pour in the batter and bake the cake in a preheated very slow oven, 275°F, for 1 hour and 30 minutes, or until a cake tester inserted in the cake comes out clean. Let the cake cool completely in the pan on a rack and turn it out onto a serving plate. Serve the cake with whipped cream sweetened and flavored with white crème de cacao to taste.

The Lyme Inn

SERVES 8 TO 10

2 cups flour
1 teaspoon baking soda
Pinch salt
1¾ cups coffee
¼ cup bourbon
5 ounces unsweetened
  chocolate
2 sticks (1 cup) butter
2 cups sugar
2 eggs, lightly beaten
1 teaspoon vanilla
Cocoa

Frozen White Chocolate & Bailey's Mousse with Warm Caramel Sauce

SERVES 6 TO 8

Frozen white chocolate and Bailey's mousse:

8 ounces white chocolate, chopped finely
6 eggs
¼ cup sugar
1 pint heavy cream
6 egg yolks (reserved)
½ cup Bailey's Irish Cream

Melt chocolate over double boiler, stirring to smooth it out. Cover and reserve in a warm place.

Separate eggs carefully, so no traces of yolk are in whites. Reserve the yolks. With an electric mixer beat whites to a frothy state (about 10 seconds); continue to beat, slowly adding sugar. Beat mixture until the whites make stiff peaks when you lift the beaters out. Reserve in refrigerator.

With electric mixer, whip until soft peaks form when the beaters are lifted out. Reserve in refrigerator.

Combine briefly with electric mixer until the yolks and Bailey's are smooth. Transfer to a double boiler and cook, stirring constantly, until the custard thickens. When the custard thickens it will happen very quickly and you must remove from the heat immediately, stirring rapidly, to keep it from breaking. If it resembles scrambled eggs it has broken and you will have to start over. If it coats the back of a spoon it is ready for the next step.

Whisk the melted white chocolate into the custard until the mixture is smooth. Fold in the egg whites gently, and then the whipped cream. Pour this into an appropriately sized container, cover tightly, and freeze for 24 hours before serving with warm caramel sauce (see next page).

New London Inn

Warm Caramel Sauce

In a heavy-bottomed saucepan over medium to low heat, mix the sugar, water, and lemon juice, stirring constantly until they have melted and turned an amber color (5 to 10 minutes).

6 ounces sugar
1 tablespoon water
¼ teaspoon lemon juice
¾ cup heavy cream
2 tablespoons butter

Remove the pan from the heat and add heavy cream. (Be careful! Stand back as you are doing so as it might spatter. It is normal for it to react violently, but keep stirring.) If the sauce is not smooth, return it to the heat, stirring, until the lumps disappear.

With the pan off the heat, add butter, and stir until it disappears. The sauce is ready for use, but can be kept warm until you are ready to serve it. It can also be refrigerated and heated up for use at a later date.

Assembly: To assemble dessert, ladle ¼ cup of sauce onto six plates. Add 3 scoops of frozen mousse. Garnish with whipped cream, strawberry, and fresh mint if desired. Serve immediately.

New London Inn

Pumpkin Cheesecake

SERVES 8

3 eight-ounce packages
  cream cheese (softened)
6 graham crackers,
  crumbled
2 cups brown sugar
6 eggs
2 cups canned or fresh
  pumpkin
¼ teaspoon cloves
¼ teaspoon nutmeg
½ teaspoon cinnamon
1 tablespoon vanilla

Butter sides and bottom of a springform pan. Shake graham cracker crumbs on sides and bottom. Refrigerate pan while mixing ingredients.

Beat ingredients above with an electric mixer. Add the pumpkin, cloves, nutmeg, cinnamon, and vanilla, and continue beating until very creamy.

Put mixture in pan. Cover outside of pan with heavy duty foil and put springform pan into bigger pan that has 1 inch of very hot water in it.

Bake at 375°F for 1½ hours. Test with toothpick or clean knife, inserted in center; cake is done when comes out dry. Cool at room temperature. Refrigerate for 3 or 4 hours.

Kedron Valley Inn

Maple Mousse

SERVES 4

1 tablespoon gelatin
½ cup water
4 egg yolks
1 cup maple syrup
½ cup light brown sugar
4 egg whites, whipped
2 cups heavy cream,
  whipped

Combine gelatin, water, egg yolks, and maple syrup over heat in a double boiler. Use a wire whip to stir out the lumps. Add the brown sugar and continue to whip. Take off heat and allow to cool slightly. Fold in the beaten egg whites and the whipped cream. Pour into champagne glasses and chill.

The Lyme Inn

Chocolate Terrine

Scald 2 cups cream. Melt chocolate in double boiler over gently simmering water. Stir in scalded cream. Pour half of mixture into 8 x 4-inch loaf pan. Refrigerate chocolate in loaf pan until firm. Transfer remaining chocolate to bowl and refrigerate.

Preheat oven to 325°F. Line baking sheet with parchment. Beat whites with salt until soft peaks form. Gradually add sugar and beat to stiff peaks. Fold in ½ cup chopped almonds. Spread mixture on prepared sheet. Bake meringue until golden brown around edges, about 15 minutes. Cool completely; meringue will fall. Cut two 8 x 4-inch pieces of meringue. Invert one piece of meringue over chocolate in loaf pan; remove paper.

Sprinkle gelatin over ¼ cup cream in heavy small saucepan and scald. Purée remaining almonds with butter in processor. Blend in gelatin mixture. Turn into large bowl. Beat remaining whipping cream to stiff peaks. Fold into gelatin mixture. Smooth over meringue in pan. Refrigerate until almond cream is firm.

Invert second meringue over almond cream; remove paper. Set aside ½ cup of chocolate in bowl. Using electric mixer, beat remaining chocolate until soft peaks form and color lightens. Spread atop meringue. Refrigerate until chocolate is firm.

To unmold, dip bottom of pan briefly into hot water. Invert terrine onto platter. Melt reserved ½ cup chocolate. Drizzle over terrine. Cut into thin slices to serve.

Hemingway's

SERVES 8 TO 10

3 cups whipping cream
1 pound imported
  semisweet chocolate
4 egg whites,
  room temperature
Pinch of salt
½ cup sugar
¾ cup chopped almonds
1 tablespoon unflavored
  gelatin
½ cup (1 stick) unsalted
  butter, room temperature

Chocolate Macadamia Truffle Torte

SERVES 8 TO 12

1 nine-inch springform
pan
6 eggs
½ pound sweet butter,
unsalted
1 pound semisweet
chocolate
1 cup macadamia nuts,
lightly roasted
1 tablespoon
Grand Marnier

✿

CHAMPAGNE WOULD BE A
TERRIFIC ACCOMPANIMENT.

Preheat oven to 450°F. Melt butter and chocolate in double boiler, stirring with wooden spoon until mixed. Remove from heat. Whip eggs until lemon colored approximately 90 seconds.

Roast nuts in 350°F oven 10 minutes or until light brown. Cool and chop. Add eggs to chocolate mix, add nuts and Grand Marnier, and mix until smooth. Pour into 9-inch springform pan that has been brushed with butter lightly and floured. Excess flour is tapped out by holding pan upside down and lightly tapping on edge of table. Make a parchment paper circle to fit bottom of pan. Insert and brush lightly with butter. Wrap aluminum foil around bottom and sides of springform pan to prevent water from seeping in. Place pan in water bath ¼ way up side of springform pan. Use hot water.

Place in 450°F oven for 5 minutes. After 5 minutes, cover with another piece of foil loosely fitted and continue cooking for another 10 minutes. Remove from oven and water bath and let cool for 3 to 4 hours or until firm. Torte will seem runny when it first comes out. This is to be expected. Cut with hot knife. Top with whipped cream or serve with raspberry or strawberry sauce.

Kedron Valley Inn

Vacherin Glace

This dessert may be served with either hot chocolate or cold raspberry sauces.

Meringues: Preheat oven to 200°F. Place egg whites and sugar in a warm mixing bowl, stirring slowly by hand until sugar is dissolved. With an electric mixer, slowly whip egg whites. Gradually increase speed until stiff peaks form. Place mixture in a pastry bag fitted with ⅜-inch star tip. Pipe 2½-inch circles, ⅓-inch thick, onto baking sheet dusted with flour or covered with parchment paper. Bake in oven for at least 4 hours. Meringues can be kept for several weeks in an airtight container.

Ice cream: Cut ice cream into 2-inch cubes and shape into 2-inch diameter cylinders.

Chocolate sauce: Combine coffee and brandy in a small saucepan and heat over low flame. Reduce by half. In another saucepan, heat cream to boiling point. Put chocolate in coffee and brandy mixture and pour in cream. Stir until smooth. Keep sauce warm until ready to serve.

Raspberry sauce: Purée raspberries in a food processor and strain. Sweeten with sugar and kirsch.

Whipped cream: In a large bowl, whip cream and vanilla extract until stiff peaks form. Place in a pastry bag fitted with ⅜-inch star tip.

To prepare, place ice cream cylinder between two meringue rounds, flat side out, and roll in almonds until coated. (This can be done up to 2 days ahead of serving and kept in airtight containers in freezer.) On a dessert plate, arrange meringues and ice cream. Decorate plate with whipped cream and pipe a crown around the top edge of meringue. Drizzle warm chocolate sauce or the raspberry sauce on dessert before serving.

SERVES 8

16 two-and-a-half inch round meringues[1]
24 ounces vanilla ice cream
⅔ cup sliced almonds, lightly toasted[1]
8 ounces whipped cream
1 cup chocolate sauce or raspberry sauce

[1]Can be prepared ahead of time.

Meringues:
5 large egg whites
1 cup sugar

Whipped Cream:
8 ounces heavy cream
½ teaspoon vanilla extract

Sauce:
(Chocolate)
1 ounce coffee
1 ounce brandy
4 ounces heavy cream
4 ounces bittersweet chocolate, chopped
or
(Raspberry)
1 pint fresh or frozen raspberries
Sugar to taste
1 teaspoon kirsch (optional)

Home Hill Country Inn

Apple Pie

SERVES 8 TO 10

Pie Dough:
1 teaspoon salt
3 cups pastry flour
2 ounces butter Crisco
6 ounces regular Crisco
1 teaspoon cider vinegar
½ cup apple cider

Apple Filling:
½ cup brown sugar
½ cup white sugar
4 tablespoons cornstarch
1 tablespoon cinnamon
½ teaspoon nutmeg
⅛ teaspoon allspice
1 tablespoon lemon juice
5½ cups apples—
    Cortland, Grannies,
    or MacIntosh

✿

THIS RECIPE WON THE
YANKEE MAGAZINE APPLE
PIE COMPETITION IN 1991.

Crust: Combine flour and salt. Mix in Criscos until they are pea-sized pieces. Combine the vinegar and cider and add to the flour mixture, then mix until just combined.

Roll out a top crust and a bottom crust. Place the bottom piece in a 9-inch pie tin.

Filling: Combine all ingredients and let stand for about 1 hour. Drain, reserving juices. Put the juice into a small saucepan and cook over medium heat, stirring constantly until thick and clear. Remove from heat and add the apples.

Cool completely and pour into the bottom of the pie shell. Eggwash the pie edge and place the top crust on. Tuck in the edges and seal the crust. Eggwash the outside of the crust and sprinkle with cinnamon sugar.

Bake for 10 minutes at 450°F and then turn down the oven to 350°F. Bake about 30 minutes longer, or until the crust is golden brown and thoroughly cooked.

Hanover Inn

Walnut Meringue

Oh my, oh my
we loved both
Having at Simon's
+ making
my own?

Preheat oven to 350°F. Grease and flour two 9-inch cake tins. Place wax paper circle on the bottom of each tin. Egg whites should be at room temperature. Place egg whites in bowl of electric mixer. Beat on high until frothy. Slowly add sugar (1 tablespoon at a time) until stiff and glossy peaks form.

With mixer on low, add vanilla and white vinegar and blend well. Turn mixer to high and beat for 30 seconds more.

Remove mixing bowl from stand and fold in walnuts. Divide batter evenly between two prepared pans. Bake in a preheated oven for 45 minutes or until lightly browned. Cool completely on wire racks.

Run a knife along the edge of the pan and invert onto plates. Remove wax paper rounds. On the bottom of one meringue layer, spread with ½ inch or so of unsweetened whipped cream. Place the bottom of the second meringue layer on top of whipped cream layer. Keep refrigerated until serving time. Serve with a sauce made of sweetened puréed strawberries.

Simon Pearce

SERVES 8 TO 10

8 egg whites
2¼ cups granulated
  sugar
2 cups chopped walnuts
2 teaspoons vanilla
1 teaspoon white vinegar

Dacquoise au Chocolat Meringue Nut Cake

SERVES ABOUT 8

¾ cup sugar
1¼ cup nuts (½ almonds,
   ½ filberts), browned
   in oven for
   10 minutes at 350°F
1 tablespoon cornstarch
6 egg whites
¼ teaspoon
   cream of tartar
Pinch of salt
Chocolate butter cream
1 cup heavy cream
2 tablespoons
   confectioners sugar
1 tablespoon rum

Coat 2 cookie sheets with butter and flour. Mark coating with 10-inch rings. Mix together the sugar, nuts, and cornstarch. Beat the whites with the salt and cream of tartar until stiff. Fold in the sugar and nut mixture. Work fast. Fill a pastry bag fitted with a plain tube with some of the meringue mixture. Pipe a ring on each tray. Following the outline of the ring, divide the remaining mixtures between the 2 rings and spread evenly with a spatula. The disks should be the same thickness all over. Bake in a 350°F oven for 20 to 25 minutes. Let disks set for 5 minutes, then slide off tray to wire rack. Let dry for about 30 minutes until dry and brittle. Trim edges to have perfect wheels.

Café La Fraise

Maple Apple Walnut Crisp

SERVES 6 TO 8

12 Granny Smith apples
   peeled, cored, and cut in
   thin slices
2 cups pure Vermont
   maple syrup
¾ cup flour
¼ teaspoon nutmeg
¼ teaspoon cloves
1 teaspoon cinnamon

Topping:
1 cup brown sugar
1 cup flour
1 cup oatmeal
1 cup butter
1 teaspoon cinnamon
½ teaspoon nutmeg

Mix all together the first 6 ingredients and place in a 6 x 4 x 2-inch baking dish.

In a food processor blend the topping ingredients: Mix and sprinkle on apple concoction. Cover with foil. Bake at 400°F for 45 minutes.

Kedron Valley Inn

Chocolate Butter Cream

Melt chocolate. Mix sugar and water in a saucepan. Bring to a boil and boil for 2 minutes over medium heat. Place egg yolks in the bowl of mixer. Pour in the sugar syrup on top of yolks while mixing at medium speed and beat for 5 minutes until mixture is thick and pale. Add butter, a tablespoon at a time, mixing at medium low speed until cream is smooth. Add melted chocolate and beat until smooth.

Assembly: Place one wheel on a serving plattter and, using a pastry bag fitted with a fluted tube, pipe a border all around the wheel. Place a small amount of butter cream in the middle of wheel. Combine cream, sugar, and rum. Whip until firm and arrange the cream in the middle of the wheel. Place the other wheel on top, smooth side up. Sprinkle with sugar. Decorate edges and middle with remaining chocolate butter cream. Refrigerate and serve cold. Cut with a serrated knife.

Café La Fraise

SERVES 8 TO 10

2 ounces unsweetened chocolate
1 ounce semisweet chocolate
⅓ cup confectioners sugar
¼ cup water
3 egg yolks
2 sticks sweet butter, softened

White Chocolate Cashew Cheesecake

Melt chocolate. Cream together cream cheese, sugar, and vanilla. Add chocolate to cream cheese mixture. Add eggs and cashews slowly to chocolate mixture.

Pour into 2 buttered 10-inch cake pans. Bake in a water bath until set and lightly browned on top, about 1 hour and 15 minutes.

Hanover Inn

YIELDS 2 TEN-INCH CAKES

3 pounds white chocolate
4 pounds soft cream cheese
1 pound, 5 ounces sugar
¾ ounce vanilla
8 eggs
1 pound chopped cashews

Poached Pears in Orange Sauce

YIELDS 6 PEARS

6 large pears,
    Bosc or Bartlett
2 tablespoons lemon juice
6 cups water
1½ cups and
    2 teaspoons sugar
½ teaspoon vanilla or
    one 3-inch piece
    vanilla bean
One 3-inch piece
    cinnamon stick
Zest of two oranges,
    cut into ⅛-inch
    julienne strips
2 teaspoons cornstarch
¾ cup strained
    orange juice
1 cup red currant jelly
½ cup Cointreau or
    Triple Sec liqueur
2 tablespoons brandy
¼ teaspoon
    ground cinnamon

Stir lemon juice into a large bowl of cold water. Peel and core pears, and drop into lemon water to keep from discoloring.

In a medium saucepan, combine 6 cups water, 1½ cups sugar, vanilla, and cinnamon stick, and bring to a boil. Add the pears. Simmer until pears are tender, 15 to 25 minutes. Transfer to a bowl and pour poaching liquid over pears and cool to room temperature.

In a small saucepan, blanch the julienne orange zest in boiling water for 5 minutes; drain and set aside. Mix cornstarch with 5 tablespoons of the orange juice, set aside.

In a medium saucepan, melt the jelly over medium heat. Gradually stir in the remaining orange juice. Taste and add sugar, heat until sugar dissolves. Boil mixture, stirring often, until sauce is reduced to one cup. Remove from heat, whisk in the cornstarch mixture; return to heat, whisking until sauce thickens, simmer for 3 minutes. Reduce heat to low. Stir in liqueur and brandy, simmer 2 minutes. Remove from heat and stir in the ground cinnamon and reserve orange zest. Refrigerate covered until cool, but not cold.

To serve, remove pears from poaching liquid and pat dry with paper towels. Place each pear on a serving plate and spoon orange sauce over pears. If made ahead remove pears and sauce from refrigerator 1 hour before serving.

Café La Fraise

Strawberry Soup

Combine the first 5 ingredients and simmer uncovered for 15 minutes, stirring occasionally. Add the strawberry purée and simmer for 10 minutes more, stirring frequently. Chill.

Whip the cream until just stiff; do not overwhip. Fold the whipped cream and the sour cream into the chilled berry mixture and chill.

Serve chilled with a dollop of soured cream and a sliced strawberry.

Café La Fraise

SERVES 6 TO 8

3 cups water
1½ cups red wine
1 cup sugar
¼ cup lemon juice
¼ teaspoon cinnamon
2 quarts strawberries,
  puréed
1 cup heavy cream
⅓ cup sour cream

Maple Chocolate and Walnut Pie

SERVES 8 TO 10

3 eggs
½ cup sugar
1 cup chopped walnuts
1 cup mini chocolate
   chips
½ cup pure Vermont
   maple syrup
½ cup corn syrup
1 teaspoon vanilla
   extract

Slightly beat eggs, add sugar, continue beating and add remainder of ingredients. Pour into an uncooked 8-inch pie shell, and cook at 375°F for about 45 minutes, or until chocolate bubbles.

The Lincoln Inn

✺

WINNER OF WOODSTOCK'S FIRST ANNUAL "TASTE OF VERMONT"
MAPLE FESTIVAL.

Benne Wafers

YIELDS 12 DOZEN
WAFERS

3 cups flour
¾ teaspoon salt
1½ teaspoons baking
   powder
6 cups brown sugar
1½ cups unsalted butter
6 eggs
3 teaspoons vanilla
4 cups sesame seeds

Sift together the flour, salt, and baking powder. Put aside. Cream the butter. Add the brown sugar, beat until light and fluffy. Add the eggs and vanilla. Beat well.

Stir in the dry ingredients and the sesame seeds. Chill the dough thoroughly. It keeps for a week or so in the refrigerator.

Preheat oven to 350°F for 2 to 3 minutes. Drop the dough onto greased parchment paper on cookie sheets in small teaspoonfuls. Bake 5 minutes, or until lightly browned.

Simon Pearce

Frozen Raspberry Mousse

Drain frozen raspberries, reserve juice. In a saucepan reduce the raspberry juice to ½ cup, then cool.

In a mixing bowl beat the egg yolks and sugar for 5 minutes on high speed. Add the cooled reduced juice and the Chamborg. In a separate bowl whip the cream until stiff; do not overwhip.

Fold the cream and the raspberries into the egg yolk mixture. Put into a container and freeze for 8 hours.

At Café la Fraise we usually serve the mousse in a meringue nest on a pool of raspberry sauce.

Café La Fraise

SERVES 8

8 large egg yolks
1½ cups sugar
4 eight-ounce boxes of
*   frozen raspberries*
¼ cup Chamborg
4 cups whipping cream

Irish Cordial Pie

Heat marshmallows and milk over medium heat, stirring constantly, just until marshmallows are melted. Refrigerate until thickened. Stir in liqueur and whiskey. Fold in whipped cream and instant coffee. Pour into crust. Refrigerate until set, at least 3 hours, or freeze.

Tulip Tree Inn

SERVES 8

1 chocolate cookie pie
*   shell or graham*
*   cracker pie shell*
32 large marshmallows
*   or 3 cups miniature*
*   marshmallows*
½ cup milk
1 teaspoon instant coffee
¼ cup coffee liqueur
3 tablespoons Irish
*   whiskey*
1½ cups whipping
*   cream, whipped*

Fruit Tarts with Apple Cider Sauce

Pastry Cream:
3 cups milk
1 vanilla bean
6 eggs
11 ounces sugar
1 cup flour
2 tablespoons Chartreuse

Cider Sauce:
2 cups apple cider
1 cinnamon stick
2 pinch nutmeg
2 cloves
1 tablespoon honey
½ cup maple syrup
1 orange, juice and rind
½ lemon, juice and rind
1 tablespoon cornstarch
Fresh fruit in season

Bring milk and vanilla bean to a boil. Mix eggs, sugar, and flour together. Bring milk slowly to mixture, whisking. Place back on stove and whisk vigorously until mixture gets very thick. Add Chartreuse, strain through china cap. Let cool.

Combine all ingredients except cornstarch and fresh fruit in season. Bring to a boil. Let simmer for 10 minutes. Thicken with cornstarch. Add raisins. Let cool.

To arrange: Fill your favorite tart shells with pastry cream. Arrange fruit nicely or top and drizzle cider sauce on and around the tarts.

Cortina Inn

Mudslide Pie

SERVES 8 TO 10

6 ounces graham cracker crumbs
3 ounces sugar
4 ounces melted butter
3 ounces ground walnuts
4 ounces honey
2½ pounds chocolate ice cream, softened
3 ounces Kahlua liqueur
1½ ounces Baileys Irish Cream

Mix melted butter, graham cracker crumbs, walnuts, and honey together. Press into a 9-inch pie crust pan and chill.

Mix ice cream, Kahlua, and Bailey's together and pour into shell and freeze.

Molly's Balloon

Index

*T*o order additional copies:

The book price is $19.95 plus postage and handling of $2.50.
Please send me ———— copies of GADABOUTS at $22.45 each.
Enclosed is my check for $ ————————
Please check which cover you want: Dartmouth Hall__ or Eggs__
Make checks payable to GARLIC PRESS

Name ————————————————————————
Street ————————————————————————
City ———————————————— State ——— Zip ————

Charge to VISA ——— or MASTERCARD ———
Card number ———————————————— Exp. Date ————
Name as it appears on card ————————————————

☞Telephone orders accepted.

Garlic Press
P.O. Box 222
New London, NH 03257
(603) 763-9191

CUT HERE

WE WELCOME YOUR COMMENTS AND ADDITIONS.
REMEMBER WHAT YOUR MOTHER SAID:
IF YOU DON'T HAVE ANYTHING NICE TO SAY,
DON'T SAY ANYTHING AT ALL.